DEPRESSION IN THE ELDERLY: A Behavioral Treatment Manual

Dolores Gallagher and Larry W. Thompson,

with
Gary Baffa, Chris Piatt,
LaDonna Ringering, and Vicki Stone

This monograph is published by the
Ethel Percy Andrus Gerontology Center
University of Southern California

RICHARD H. DAVIS, Ph.D.
Director of Publications and Media Projects

THE UNIVERSITY OF SOUTHERN CALIFORNIA PRESS

ISBN 0-88474-125-7

Library of Congress Catalog Number 81-66766

Managing Editor: Richard Bohen
Associate Editor: Jean Rarig

Preface

Depression, often a significant mental health problem for older persons in our society, results when individuals are unable to withstand events typically associated with advancing age: loss of spouse and friends, decline in health and vigor, and reduced income. Although most people are able to adjust to these changes, a sizable proportion of the elderly population is not, and impaired functioning results. Some individuals, particularly those with multiple losses, may become overwhelmed and experience a substantial depressive reaction.

Treatment programs for older persons have been under-utilized, as can be seen when comparing the prevalence of depression in the older age ranges and the small percentage of the elderly who are seen in mental health settings. A pessimistic view regarding the effectiveness of traditional psychotherapy with older persons on the part of mental health professionals may be partially responsible for this imbalance.

This manual describes a behavioral therapy approach to treatment of depression in older persons which is both short term and effective. The Workbook section covers in detail techniques for developing and maintaining specific coping skills to deal with depression and prevent future episodes. It is hoped that this treatment method will be used to assist this underserved older population, and will stimulate the development of additional psychotherapeutic techniques.

James E. Birren, Executive Director
Andrus Gerontology Center
University of Southern California

Authors

Gary Baffa, Ph.D. Candidate, Psychology, University of Southern California, and Lecturer, California State University at Long Beach, California

Dolores Gallagher, Ph.D., formerly Assistant Director of Adult Counseling, Andrus Gerontology Center, University of Southern California, Los Angeles, California; currently with the Geriatric Research, Education, Consultation, & Clinical Center (GRECC), Palo Alto VA Medical Center, Palo Alto, California

Chris Piatt, M.S.G., Geriatric Mental Health Specialist, Tacoma-Pierce County Comprehensive Mental Health Center, Tacoma, Washington

LaDonna Ringering, Ph.D. Candidate, Psychology, University of Southern California, and Evaluation Coordinator, Center for the Partially Sighted, Santa Monica Hospital, Santa Monica, California

Vicki Stone, Ph.D., Research Psychologist, Litigation Sciences, 655 Deep Valley Drive, Palos Verdes Peninsula, California

Larry W. Thompson, Ph.D., Professor, Psychology Department, and Director, Adult Counseling Services of the Andrus Gerontology Center, University of Southern California, Los Angeles

Acknowledgments

This work is the result of cooperative effort among the six named authors, who have been members of an ongoing treatment team concerned with use of behavioral approaches to improve symptoms of depression in elderly persons. Over a period of about one year (1979 to 1980), the authors collaborated to produce sections of this text. The senior authors assumed responsibility for integrating materials, editing, and producing a satisfactory finished product.

Supported by a small National Institute of Mental Health research grant entitled "Psychotherapy for Depression in the Elderly" (1 RO1 MH32157), three types of psychosocial treatment were compared for effectiveness in treating elderly depressives. All clients seen in the research project were diagnosed as experiencing "major depressive disorders" according to standard criteria for the field, were free from significant cognitive impairment, and were not taking psychotropic medications during the course of treatment. Behavioral psychotherapy, cognitive therapy, and brief psychotherapy (which is short term and psychodynamically oriented) were employed and compared.

Follow-ups have indicated that both behavioral and cogntive treatment were superior to brief psychotherapy at three months, six months, and one year, although all three techniques had been regarded as equally beneficial immediately upon termination of treatment. In addition, clients in the behavioral group seemed in some respects to show more improvement than clients in cognitive therapy: for example, somewhat fewer relapses over the first six months of follow-up and somewhat lower scores on the various depression measures used. However, there were significantly more dropouts in behavioral therapy in the early stages of treatment than in the other two modalities. This appears to have been due to a self-selection factor; clients who were unable to accept the behavioral treatment rationale tended to drop out early, and those who chose to complete the program reflected this attitudinal factor in their subsequent improvement.

We are deeply indebted to Dr. Lewinsohn and his colleagues at the University of Oregon. Their detailed behavioral treatment manual (Lewinsohn and Grosscup, 1978) provided us with a basic structure from which to proceed in designing a behavioral treatment method for older persons. We have highlighted some aspects of the original manual, shifted emphasis in some areas, and developed a number of original contributions which are reflected in the pages of this text. Dr. Lewinsohn's help in staff training, problem solving, and consultation has been invaluable.

Based on our experience in this project, we feel certain that appropriate use of behavioral techniques can substantially reduce the negative consequences of modererate to severe depression in the upper age ranges. We hope this manual will provide sufficient information to permit behavioral treatment for older adults to be added to the clinical repertoire. Because demographic information indicates that approximately 20 percent of the population in the year 2000 will be in the over-60 age range, clinicians need to be sensitized to the special mental health needs of older persons.

This manual represents a beginning in efforts to treat depression in the elderly through behavioral therapy. Modification and refinement may be required as new clinical issues emerge. The authors will welcome information on uses of behavioral therapy from those who employ the method in practice and from those whose approach varies from that outlined in the text.

Dolores Gallagher, Ph.D.
Los Angeles, California
March 1981

Contents

I.

BACKGROUND

AND

OVERVIEW

1 An Introduction to Behavioral Treatment for Depression in the Elderly

DEMOGRAPHICS OF DEPRESSION

Depression is one of the most serious mental health problems among older adults. As many as 10 percent of adults of all ages experience serious depression (Silverman, 1968), but the occurrence is even more frequent among the ever increasing population of older adults. Estimates of depression in persons over age 60 have ranged from 10 to 65 percent (Epstein, 1976). Conservative estimates of depression in older persons without physical health problems have been placed at 4 to 6 percent (Gurland, 1976). The figures for those with physical ailments accompanying depression are considerably higher. Salzman and Shader (1979) report that the prevalence of depression in individuals with physical ailments common to the elderly (e.g., cardiovascular disease, cancer, diabetes) ranges between 10 and 40 percent, depending on the type of illness. In some instances physical problems in the elderly may trigger depression, while in others somatic complaints may stem from depression. Gerner (1979) has provided a concise review of the epidemiology of depression in older adults.

Despite the high prevalence of depression in the older population, few of the elderly are seen in mental health settings when compared with the young (Redick & Taube, 1980). Several explanations have been advanced for the low utilization of mental health services by the elderly. Clinicians tend to avoid working with older individuals because they either have found them difficult to treat or have accepted the negative stereotype that older adults show minimal benefits from psychotherapy (Butler & Lewis, 1977). Also, many older individuals frankly report that they themselves are reluctant to seek treatment because of the intense social stigma or because receiving treatment would stand as a clear indication that they are "losing their mind." Finally, identification of depression in the elderly may be overlooked because of frequent emphasis on somatic complaints suggesting organic involvement.

As a result of these factors, special attention is required for treatment of older persons. First, treatable depression should not be overlooked because of diagnostic complications. Second, personal prejudices may interfere with the prognosis for mental health problems in the elderly. Third, special effort should be made to offset fears or stereotyped notions which might prevent the elderly client from seeking mental health treatment. The information in this book should help with the first and second of these points, and if so, the third will be resolved.

IDENTIFYING DEPRESSION

Depression, a complex syndrome, can be difficult to diagnose accurately and treat appropriately at any age. It is manifested in a great variety of ways with different individuals. Older persons typically report wide ranges of complaints and differing combinations of symptoms which are associated with depression in younger age groups: dysphoria, somatic symptoms (including sleeplessness or loss of appetite), social interaction problems, help-seeking behaviors, and motivational difficulties associated with routine tasks of daily living.

A number of the somatic symptoms typically associated with depression in younger individuals can occur with regularity in the elderly as a result of other age-related complications. On the other hand, somatic complaints presented by older depressed individuals may also hint at possible organic involvement and need for appropriate medical evaluation.

As a result, the problem of diagnosing depression is more complicated in the elderly than in the young. Careful evaluation is essential—first, to identify that depression is in fact present, and then to evaluate what is likely to be causing the depressed mood. This sets the stage for developing an appropriate treatment plan.

In Chapter 5, several methods of evaluating the presence of depression in the elderly will be discussed. More detailed technical information on diagnosis is contained in numerous sources (Raskin

& Jarvik, 1979; Dessonville, Gallagher, Thompson, & Finnell, 1980; Popkin, Gallagher, Thompson, & Moore, 1980; Gurland, 1976; Epstein, 1976; Zarit, 1980).

WHY THE BEHAVIORAL APPROACH?

In many clinics throughout the country, typical approaches to the treatment of depression in the elderly rely heavily on supportive therapy, psychoactive drugs, or some combination of both. Many leading theorists in the field of depression argue that supportive therapy should not be the treatment of choice for depression in young and middle age adults (Beck, Rush, Shaw, & Emery, 1979; Lewinsohn, 1974, 1975; Rehm, 1977), and there is every reason to believe that this is the case for older adults. Research at the Andrus Gerontology Center has provided documentation for this position (Gallagher & Thompson, 1980).

There has also been some question about the efficacy of pharmacotherapy when compared with cognitive (Rush, Beck, Kovacs, & Hollon, 1977; Kovacs, Rush, Beck, & Hollon, 1981) and structured interpersonal (Weissman, Klerman, Prusoff, Sholomskas, & Padian, 1981) approaches to the treatment of depression. While drugs may or may not be effective in reducing symptoms, there are problems in using antidepressant medication with the elderly; non-compliance, increased risk of side effects, and increased complications due to polypharmacy are all known to occur.

In view of these findings, it is not surprising that many professionals hold a pessimistic view about the usefulness of traditional mental health approaches for treating depression in the elderly (Levy, Derogatis, Gallagher, & Gatz, 1980). Useful treatment alternatives are needed. Our research has shown that behavioral techniques can be extremely effective in treating depression in many elderly clients.

The approach presented here has been based primarily on the theoretical and empirical work of Lewinsohn and his colleagues at the University of Oregon (Lewinsohn, 1974; Lewinsohn, Sullivan, & Grosscup, 1980). Lewinsohn's particular variation of behavioral theory stresses the functional relationships between current everyday life events and depression. Inherent in that theory is the concept of identifying reasons for a client's depression and defining related goals for therapy. Intermediate goals are particularly emphasized to establish indicators of gradual improvement in the level of depression.

Over the years Lewinsohn and his associates have carefully evaluated two sets of conditions likely to precede and to sustain depressive episodes of clinical proportions in young adults:

(1) reduced rate of response-contingent positive reinforcement (this occurs primarily through reduction in number of pleasant activities and/or increase in number of unpleasant activities) and (2) reduction of instrumental social skills that permit individuals to obtain these positive reinforcements in their environments.

The importance of an additional factor, self-reinforcement, noted by other behaviorally oriented therapists such as Fuchs and Rehm (1977), is also emphasized in our approach. Because depressed persons often fail to adequately reinforce themselves, self-reward strategies need to be strengthened. Since the environmental and social context is often far less accommodating for the elderly, the therapist needs to exert special effort and creativity to insure that the older person will experience success with self-reward attempts. This point will be discussed in some detail in later chapters.

The behavioral treatment outlined in this manual builds on the prior work of these psychologists, including their own treatment manuals (Lewinsohn & Grosscup, 1978; Rehm, 1977). Our contribution has been to modify existing approaches to improve their efficacy with older depressives, and to develop new strategies based on insights from our clinical work. It is recommended that the reader become familiar with the primary sources cited above for detailed presentations of behavioral theory and principles beyond the scope of this manual.

Behavioral Therapy as a Model for Self-Change

Behavioral approaches to treatment of depression have been effective primarily because they establish a systematic process for self-change. A recent longitudinal study (Vaillant, 1977) has confirmed the fact that people who plan their time and follow through are happier in their adult years and seem to live longer. This ability to be practical-minded and organized in planning and use of time seems related to positive adaptation to aging. Therefore, systematic application of such strategies through behaviorally oriented treatment should be valuable in initial recovery from depression and subsequent prevention of future episodes.

The value of initiating a self-change process with an older depressed individual is two-fold. First, older persons experience a great deal of stress which typically increases with the years; learning self-change principles should contribute to better adaptation to stresses. Second, and perhaps even more important, it is through this experiential process of self-change that clients can best improve their feelings of self-efficacy (Bandura, 1977). This is an important ingredient in motivating clients to continue using skills that they learn in therapy.

The Need for a Behavioral Treatment Manual

Although it might be assumed that a treatment plan based on systematic analysis, careful monitoring, and appropriate skills training should be able to reduce depression in older persons, general behavioral approaches have been unsuccessful in many cases.

A straightforward application of behavioral principles often fails to allow for the varied and complex special needs of older depressed persons. For example, many elders experience a genuine decline in pleasant activity level accompanied by a real increase in unpleasant events. In addition, through no fault of their own, elders' opportunities to obtain social reinforcement from others are often reduced because the number of people to whom they can relate has been decreasing.

Faced with the harshness of these realities, it sometimes is easy for both client and therapist alike to become disenchanted with techniques that can be insensitive to unique factors involved in the origins of depression in the later decades of life. To promote positive change, the treatment program must be carefully tailored to the specific context and situation of each elderly person seeking help.

The purpose of this manual is to aid clinicians in their efforts to apply a range of behavioral techniques to their older clients. Detailed steps for treatment outlined in Part IV, "Session by Session Workbook for Behavioral Treatment of Depression," are based on successful strategies which emerged during a two-year period of research and development of behavioral treatment at the Andrus Gerontology Center of the University of Southern California. The manual should also help other therapists to avoid problems encountered during this period of experimentation.

STEPS IN TREATMENT

The aim of behavioral treatment is to develop a generic set of skills for coping with depression, and this requires that the client interact with his environment to produce concrete changes. He usually must learn new instrumental behaviors so that he can operate effectively on his environment. This process includes a number of steps; five major ones are outlined below to help with orientation to the overall program:

1. The individual client must learn to examine his day-by-day activities to focus attention on what he is doing in relation to the world. This is best done by monitoring or observing behavior. Clients are taught to monitor their moods as well.

Clients frequently see themselves as passive recipients of the effects of events or hurts which have originated in the world outside themselves; they may say, "I never realized that I got depressed every Sunday morning, or every evening around six o'clock." Monitoring seems to have a positive impact on depressed people, because it allows them to examine their activities and consider how the activities and certain moods may be related.

2. The client will need to be helped to see the relationship between moods and activity level. The client needs to comprehend the fact that moods are related to behavior. Frequently this will elicit an "aha experience"; once this relationship has been established, treatment can focus on acquiring skills—skills needed either to increase pleasant activities or to decrease the impact of unpleasant ones.

This skill in recognizing mood/activity relationships, although easy to describe, is difficult to accomplish, yet very meaningful to the client once it has occurred. Everyone can learn to monitor, and with enough trials most clients can learn to see the relationship between moods and actions. In our experience it is not beyond the reach of most persons, even seriously depressed individuals, to learn these techniques.

3. When the client has reached a clear understanding of the connection between mood and activity, therapist and client will be ready to share the task of selecting aspects of the client's life that should be changed. Most older persons cannot change the fact that they have a chronic physical illness or the reality that their income has been reduced to perhaps half of what it formerly was. Still, the response can be something other than depression. An alternative is constructive activity. The individual can learn what pursuits are possible despite physical limitations, or can seek part time employment to augment income. A great deal of trial and error may be required to identify activities that are significant and have potential for change, but once they have been pinpointed, change can be produced through systematic behavioral practices.

4. Once the client has identified and worked on changing certain activities, the next step is to begin to assume more self-initiated changes. As a sense of effectiveness develops and success is experienced with greater frequency, motivation to assume other changes that will promise positive benefits will increase; successful experiences encourage repetition and stimulate additional plans.

5. The final learning step involves generalization or transfer of skills learned to multiple situations in one's everyday world. For some clients, this is the most difficult part of the process, even though they have learned behavioral principles and skills in the therapy sessions. Typically, it is achieved during follow-up periods when the client is functioning primarily on his own with minimal therapist contact. We recommend periodic booster sessions

following termination of formal treatment for a period of three to six months. These booster sessions provide opportunities for the client to discuss successful and unsuccessful use of behavioral strategies as well as to problem-solve about new situations that may have developed in the interim.

THE THERAPIST'S ROLE:
EDUCATOR AND COLLABORATOR

In order to accomplish the preceding treatment steps, the therapist needs to define his role as primarily that of an educator and collaborator. This involves taking an active rather than a passive stance toward the client, as well as willingness to be flexible at different stages of treatment. For example, being direct is essential in early treatment sessions, while increasing emphasis on the collaborative nature of therapy is fruitful in the middle and late stages.

The therapist's teaching function may be unpopular with some clinicians (even those with a behavioral orientation) who are unaccustomed to working within the degree of structure promoted in this manual. In fact, a number of therapists in training at the University of Southern California were initially reluctant to use this approach, considering it "too mechanical." However, most older clients have found it useful to proceed through most or all of the areas covered in the Workbook, Section IV. Time required for each segment should be adjusted appropriately for individual clients.

Novice behavioral therapists tend to fear that clients will not have enough time in a given session to talk about what is particularly salient that week, or that the sessions will be so occupied with forms, homework, etc., that there will be no time for "talk" (i.e., for therapy in the traditional sense). All sessions have been structured to insure some "talk time" at every meeting. This is especially important in order to maintain adequate therapeutic rapport with older persons, who may have few other supportive persons in their daily lives.

There are a number of other ways to develop a good collaborative relationship. These include attentiveness and careful listening so that the client's actual words can be used when appropriate to make certain points clearer; frequent requests for clarification of what the client means when new information is presented or problems are experienced; frequent eliciting of feedback to determine if the client is grasping what you are saying or needs further amplification; and finally, flexibility in a number of areas such as setting appointment times, designing homework assigments, and creatively encouraging generalization of principles learned.

Promoting self-reliance in older persons is a significant part of treatment, and to accomplish this the therapist's interpersonal skillsa re as important as technical expertise. Material spontaneously reported by the client in a session can be effectively adapted by therapists to demonstrate behavioral techniques and assign homework.

Considerable interpersonal skill is also needed to initially engage clients in treatment and to provide a supportive atmosphere that encourages them to continue. It is wise to avoid being so rigidly consumed following structure that important information is missed or is not woven effectively into the structure of the session.

Finally, accepting the educative and collaborative functions central to this therapy is necessary. Therapists who believe in the primacy of emotional release or interpretation or long term insight-oriented therapy often find it difficult to adapt to the role requirements involved in behavioral therapy. The therapist's "comfort level" as treatment proceeds will provide a good indicator: significant discomfort on his part and/or radical departure from the treatment protocol can signal a potential for role-related problems that should be addressed before much additional behavioral therapy is attempted.

SUMMARY

Psychotherapy has long been overlooked as a treatment for depression in the elderly. This is partly because traditional approaches have been relatively ineffective. Alternative treatments are sorely needed. Highly structured behavioral therapy has proven effective in treatment of many depressed older adults. Successful treatment depends on several key ingredients: the therapist's familiarity with the treatment package, willingness to proceed through the designated steps, and conviction that this approach will be useful with specific clients.

2 The Self-Change Process

DEVELOPING A PLAN FOR SELF-CHANGE

Behavioral therapy is basically a process of client self-change which is structured by therapist and client collaboratively and which proceeds through several steps or phases. This emphasis on self-change is based on the idea that successful change is more likely to occur when a plan relevant to an individual's everyday life situation is implemented. A number of discrete steps are involved in helping the client to develop a self-change program, according to Lewinsohn, Munoz, Youngren, and Zeiss (1978); they are:

1. Pinpoint the problem.
2. Learn to self-monitor.
3. Identify the antecedents or events that typically precede the depression.
4. Identify the events of consequences that may occur after the depression is experienced.
5. Set a goal for change.
6. Self-contract for changes; provide rewards for any changes accomplished.
7. Evaluate the effectiveness of the self-change plan, and modify the goal if necessary.
8. Generalize the utility of the particular plan and strategies learned to other everyday life problems.

However, several problems may be encountered when one attempts to apply the above schema to depressed older adults. First, the idea of self-change is not always readily accepted by older depressives. It is common for clients to say, "Yes, I want to feel better, but I don't really want to put in the effort involved."

> A 68-year-old retired teacher, a potential client for behavioral therapy, strongly resisted the idea that she could effect change in herself; she wanted to improve only by taking medication of various sorts.

Other clients may resist, not the overall concept, but one of the specific steps in the self-change process such as learning to monitor everyday behavior or setting a concrete goal for change. For example, deciding what behaviors the older depressed client should monitor is often a time-consuming and frustrating process. Self-monitoring techniques will be ineffective if they are too "global," yet many older persons resist monitoring specific behaviors that are likely to lead to improvement.

> Mrs. X, a 60-year-old married woman, complained of repeated "anxiety attacks" that occurred when she felt threatened because of some change in her husband's physical health status. He was a man with a history of several major heart attacks. Every time he complained of a pain in his chest, this client believed it was a sign of an impending heart attack and thus became panicky. However, she did not want to monitor her response; she felt that, given the circumstances, it was a sensible response. She also would not agree with the therapist on a goal of reducing the frequency of these panic attacks (which represented her way of showing how much she cared). Only by involving her husband in the treatment plan was it possible to gain her cooperation in tracking, developing positive goals, and learning more adaptive ways to respond to the husband's complaints of chest pains. She eventually learned to monitor how often she asked him about the pains, to ask her husband's opinion as to whether he felt they signified an impending heart attack, and to relax so that in a true emergency situation she could act more effectively.

Finally, it is often difficult for older clients to set realistic goals for change. Frequently multiple problems are present, some of which cannot be resolved through psychotherapy, and the client does not know where to begin or what to aim for.

> Mr. Y, a 72-year-old married man, reported marital difficulties, financial concerns, fear of physical health decline, and difficulty in sleeping. His physical health problems and financial concerns tended to create transportation problems

which needed to be tackled first, for they were obstacles to securing treatment. The financial concerns most likely could not be dealt with in therapy, and the fear of health decline would need to be checked through consultation with his physician to determine whether it was realistic. This left his marital problems and sleep problems as potential targets for behavioral treatment. It took several appointments to sort out these issues so that behavioral therapy could begin.

The following suggestions will concretize the self-change process outlined above so that it can be applied more effectively with older clients.

Pinpointing the Problem

All of the problems described—social, psychological, and medical—will appear to the client to be interrelated. By himself, he will be unable to differentiate those problems which behavioral therapy can help versus those that are not amenable to this approach. Both Mrs. X and Mr. Y represent a number of older clients who really need help in differentiating their problems and redefining them as to (1) problems related to what the client himself is actually doing—not things being done to him—and (2) problems that are in some way under his control.

Self-Monitoring

Older clients have great difficulty completing forms, which have usually been designed with younger persons in mind and therefore have small boxes, small print that is difficult to read, and often insufficient accompanying explanation to insure that they will be completed correctly. Examples of forms used in the U.S.C. project have been supplied in the Appendix as suggestions. The therapist may wish to modify forms for a particular client. A blind client would be unable to complete any of these forms, but could self-monitor using a tape recorder; an individual with hearing loss but less visual problem could benefit from instructions typed in large letters and attached to all forms to save frequent repetition by the therapist.

Identifying Antecedents and Consequences

Clients are often unable to identify events that have preceded their depression; they usually cannot relate behavioral consequences clearly either, especially when the depression is severe. Family members or friends can help clarify these sequences of events. Diagramming the sequences can be very helpful when identifying what led to specific depressive feelings and what resulted from them.

Setting Goals

Goals should be set in a stepwise fashion. Early goals should be relatively small and likely to be accomplished, thus insuring some success experiences which will encourage the client to proceed.

Self-Contracting and Self-Rewards

Many older individuals almost refuse to reward themselves for progress, reflecting the attitude that people are not entitled to a reward for just doing what they have been told to do or are supposed to do. Others consider the whole idea "downright silly," and "something for kids to do." In other cases, this position may reflect a long-standing personality pattern, and debates are usually futile. Often the therapist can get such clients to try self-reward just as an experiment to see if it affects their mood. Finding an illustration in their past experience where they tried something they thought was "dumb" and it worked out well frequently encourages them to go along with the idea. Testimonials also help; a 71-year-old lady reported:

> I thought the idea of rewarding yourself for doing something was the craziest thing I ever heard of, but, by gosh, it works—it really works! Now when I run up against something I don't want to do, I tell myself if I don't do it I'll feel bad, but if I do it then I can let myself take Barbara, my granddaughter, out to lunch and an early movie. That seems to give me that extra little push I need to get started, and then once I'm going I usually can get it done.

We emphasize this point strongly, because for those individuals who can learn to self-reward, therapy seems to proceed more quickly.

Evaluating Effectiveness and Generalizing

These steps usually require therapist assistance, since the client cannot easily figure out what is going right or wrong about a particular self-change plan. Again, as noted earlier, older clients tend to think in global terms and see their problems as interrelated, so analysis of strengths and weaknesses of specific attempts at change are difficult. Also, older clients may need time to acquire the various skills necessary to reach their goals because they are out of practice. For example, elderly individuals who live alone may be satisfied in some ways despite the lack of social interaction in their lives. Initiating social contact (for example, in a senior citizens' club) may be very frightening for them. Since most social skills get rusty with infrequent use, the therapist should encourage the client to role play in the treatment session and practice with supportive individuals in order to gain confidence to move out into a larger social world. This last step, generalization of the learned skill, is the most difficult to achieve. Frequently several appointments and creative homework assignments are necessary to begin the generalization process.

COMMITMENT BY CLIENT TO SELF-CHANGE

A client's commitment to the self-change process can best proceed when three elements come together: (1) willingness to learn self-change skills, (2) behavioral indications of motivation to change, and (3) ability to prioritize daily activities to create time for oneself. A deficiency in any one of these areas will impede progress.

Will Power in Relation to Self-Change

Older depressed adults often take the view that they are depressed because they are lacking in will power or because they no longer have the energy to change. This perspective can only undermine efforts toward self control. If the client takes the view that the problems stem from some unalterable intrapsychic state of weakness, he will not get involved in behavioral treatment. Older clients who take this position are usually silently comparing themselves with younger people or others whom they describe as being effective in self-control situations; these clients simultaneously rate themselves as weak in self-control tasks. An effective way to appraise this condition is to use the argument of Rimm and Masters (1974). This consists of pointing out to the client that effective self-control in others, both young and old, is not due to possession of some strength or moral fiber, but instead to a beneficial history of learning behaviors which yield personal gratification. Depressed persons' difficulties stem, not from inadequate efforts, but from lack of techniques for achieving their goals—techniques which need to be discovered and developed.

Bandura (1979) calls this concept "self-efficacy,' which means that the more the client feels a sense of self-mastery, the less likely he will feel depression. However, feelings of self-efficacy are based on positive experiences with the environment which provide gratification, as noted above. Depressives usually do not feel much of a sense of self-mastery or have positive experiences, and hence blame themselves for being too weak to do things necessary for improvement. When a client can be led to see the relationship between instrumental behavior and goal achievement, this downward spiral can be replaced by a more positive upward spiral.

Whenever will power becomes an issue in treatment, the therapist should reemphasize the importance of learning and problem solving.

> An older female client may want to discuss with her adult children how she would like to be set to rest when she dies. Each time she approaches the topic, the children dismiss her concern. After a while she feels she does not have the will power to get the children to listen to her. The therapist should help her to reframe this concern. Getting the adult children to listen can occur once effective communication and assertive skills are learned; the woman can then obtain her aims and no longer "put herself down."

Behavioral Signs of Motivation to Change

The need to obtain a client's verbal commitment to proceed with therapy has already been emphasized. Unfortunately, some clients may state that they understand and accept the rationale, yet they do not adequately comprehend it and are often too embarrassed to make this known. When clients do not thoroughly understand the reasons for exercises and tasks they are asked to perform and how these relate to their problems, they see no value in the requests and often will not comply.

To correct misconceptions and reinforce clients' understanding, it is helpful if the therapist asks the client to state in his own words what is going on in a session; then the therapist should restate the points. For example, older clients may agree that being relaxed is much more pleasant than being tense, but may not see how practice at home every evening can be instrumental in getting them out of the house and into social situations where they can become acquainted with new friends.

Understanding increases when the therapist details the progression of relaxation training and explains what should take place. First, the client should learn to be relaxed in the office, then more fully at home. After this he should learn to recognize the advantages of being relaxed in real life situations. Next, he should understand that being relaxed is incompatible with being depressed, helps to make adversive situations less adversive, and eliminates tension which hinders interpersonal satisfaction. Finally, the therapist should point out that in the relaxed state, feelings of enjoyment and competence are enhanced; that being relaxed in a social situation increases the probability that one will be more effective and enjoy it more.

Once the therapist has covered these points, the client should review them in his own words. Presentation of this logical sequence enables him to see *why* he is learning how to relax in the office, as well as the benefits that will accrue from learning these relaxation procedures well.

Some clients understand the treatment rationale, verbally commit themselves, yet do not make a full *behavioral* commitment in that they do not follow through consistently with the demands of therapy, particularly the homework. In such a case, variations in the treatment plan may be necessary to enlist the client's participation and maintain motivation; for example:

> An older client finds it difficult to record her relaxation responses throughout the day, since she practices at a senior center; her Relaxation Log is left untouched and the therapist is not sure the technique is being practised. The client should be directed to record her daily relaxation responses during the evening from memory rather than at the time of relaxation. (Other suggestions can be found in Chapter 4, Homework, under "Premature Termination.")

While the general guidelines of the treatment plan should be followed, individual differences may recommend modifications.

A client may periodically need some assistance to carry out a specific aspect of the plan. Significant others may be needed to lend a hand:

> A female client who experienced frequent anxiety attacks during the early morning initially found it impossible to practice relaxation responses and gain self-control at that time, and instead called her therapist to get reassurance until the attack subsided. A family member, willing to assist as a kind of auxiliary therapist, worked with the client to get the anxiety under control. The therapist was then called only if the attack was really severe. Instead of reassuring the client, the therapist would immediately begin to guide the client to doing the relaxation exercise over the phone. Assisted in this way, the client was able to hang up the phone and continue the exercises, thus gaining self-control with minimal intervention from the therapist.

Priority of Time for Oneself

Commitment to behavioral treatment is a commitment to self. In making the commitment, a client gives himself permission to free time for himself—time to attend sessions, and time to work between sessions. Not all clients will give therapy the priority it deserves, particularly with respect to time, as will be evidenced when initially arranging appointments. A number of other activities may compete for the available time slots.

The client will need to be educated by the therapist to understand that therapy must have a high priority, with less important things rescheduled. Such reordering will confirm that the client is beginning to take control over his life, and thus make life better for himself.

Depressed clients not only have difficulty allowing themselves to reserve time for treatment sessions, but often have problems scheduling homework time. This may reflect feelings of uneasiness or guilt which tend to arise as progress is made. Other behavioral signs are clues to this discomfort: coming late for appointments, missing appointments altogether, or attempting to space them too far apart. Such delays can retard progress of treatment and make it difficult. This hurdle can usually be overcome by pointing out that through such behaviors the client is robbing himself of learning time which contributes to eventual relief of depressive symptoms; also, by acknowledging that positive change initially feels awkward to most people.

Other events may conflict periodically with scheduling of meetings (a new health problem requiring a physician's visit is common with older persons, for example). While reasons for rescheduling an appointment may be legitimate, it is wise to point out that commitment to the time involved is basically a commitment to self-change and to providing conditions for improvement. In short, insist that the client give therapy time and homework time high priorities.

SUMMARY

In this chapter we have stressed the importance of viewing commitment to behavioral therapy as a commitment to changing oneself. A number of ways to encourage this process have been presented, along with problems that may be encountered when presenting the concept to older adults. Specifically, attitudinal and behavioral barriers have been reviewed, and emphasis has been placed on the need to prioritize activities so that adequate time can be spent each day on treatment-related issues.

It is critical to effectively communicate the ideas in this chapter. Some initial resistance can be anticipated, but an experimental attitude should be encouraged so that the client comes to realize that behavioral treatment is intended to set in motion a self-change process. Ultimately, this should prove to be of greater benefit to the client than more traditional forms of treatment which do not focus on this aspect of mental health.

3 Contextual Factors Affecting Therapy

CONTEXTUAL FACTORS AFFECTING THERAPY

Before going further into the technical aspects of treatment, the therapist needs to be sensitized to several situational factors which often influence the progress of treatment with older depressives. If unrecognized or unacknowledged, these factors can and do sabotage efforts to make changes. Accordingly, they should be discussed in the early phases of therapy—when problems are being defined, and *before* strategies for change have been devised. Four problem areas are particularly important in relation to behavioral treatment with older adults; (1) socioeconomic and cultural factors, (2) the role of the family, (3) medical complications, and (4) financial problems.

SOCIOECONOMIC AND CULTURAL FACTORS

An extensive handbook listing factors affecting responsiveness to psychotherapy and behavior change has been compiled by Garfield and Bergin (1978). The influence of socioeconomic and cultural factors can be seen in the well-documented fact that middle-class, well-educated, verbal clients have had the most successful therapeutic results from treatment. This finding implies that there may be problems in work with older adults who as a group have

relatively lower levels of education, sophistication, a
logical awareness. Therefore, it may be necessary to
optimism within both client and therapist as concerns are
reframed along behavioral lines. Behavioral therapy has
successful with older depressives (Gallagher, in press; Knight, 19
Thompson & Gallagher, 1980) partially because it emphasizes
learning concrete new patterns of action, rather than broad
personality change.

Some cultural values and mores which are specific to certain
subgroups can surface differences of opinion between therapist and
client as to appropriate behavior—for example, the issue of
assertiveness:

> A Mexican American woman in her late fifties was having
> relationship problems in her marriage, yet when the therapist
> suggested that some modified assertiveness training would be
> appropriate in this instance, the client felt this was a very poor
> suggestion. Both she and her husband held the view that men
> have more rights than women.

By taking the time to become familiar with acceptable and
unacceptable patterns within a particular subgroup, the therapist
can avoid alienating a client and can increase his sensitivity to the
parameters of likely change.

The elderly also come from cohorts that are different and
unique. During their formative years, rules more stringent than
those found in society today were in force. The fact that the majority
of persons over age sixty have value structures of earlier cultural
cohorts influences how the elderly define problems and respond to
therapy. Many older clients do not want to talk about sexual
problems in treatment despite the fact that these may be salient.
Many older clients resist making assertive responses considered
appropriate by most people today because assertiveness can be
mistaken for rudeness. Elders' expectations for contact with family
members may not coincide with middle-aged children's expectations—another cohort issue. Time to discuss these changing social
norms with clients can be a very helpful aspect of treatment in itself.

There is probably more diversity than similarity among elderly
people in these cultural and cohort differences. Individual
differences in personality are, in fact, far more common than any
uniform global traits (Botwinick, 1978). Rather than generalize here
about a number of possible value clashes, behavioral therapists
should look carefully at the historical and contextual backgrounds
of their clients and endeavor to learn what values prevail. While
there may be broad attitudinal changes in such things as sexuality,
women's roles, intergenerational contact, and assertiveness, it is

nost elderly individuals are conservative
e the therapist must proceed cautiously
s. Older individuals can and do change
ly this proceeds in small and sometimes

LY FACTORS

....pics, the family of a client can affect treatment
participation. Older clients come to the therapy setting already
involved in established relationships and family dynamics that have
a complex history. Within each family network, members have
evolved a system of rewards, a hierachy of power distribution, and
entrenched family roles. For example, older individuals who are
dependent on existing family members for social interaction may
fear "rocking the boat" because they are unlikely to be able to replace
these significant family relationships.

Given the diversity of today's families, it is important to obtain
as much information as possible about each client's family structure
at the outset of treatment. Knowledge of the family constellation
can assist in setting reasonable treatment goals and foster greater
understanding of each client as an individual. If the person is
married, the marriage is usually longstanding, and patterns and
habits of relating are probably firmly established. On the other
hand, many older women are widowed; this fact often provides a
unique context for therapy. Most older individuals will probably
have adult children to contend with, therefore the family problems
will be different from those of a younger family. In other cases, very
old parents who are still living would present different problems.

The perceptive therapist is wise to elicit from the family their
attitudes toward the client's depression and toward the potential for
beneficial treatment effects. Expectations of a client's family
members can directly facilitate or sabotage the therapeutic effort.
Some clients have been urged to try behavioral treatment by adult
children who have defined the problem in a way that has led them to
feel psychotherapy could bring about a solution, yet the parent may
not be sure this is the case. The family can be "for" therapy, the
client "against."

> A 63-year-old woman was brought in by her daughter, who did
> most of the talking with the therapist in the intake appoint-
> ment. The daughter felt the mother had been depressed since
> the father's death ten years earlier. According to the daughter,
> Mom did not have enough to keep her occupied, watched far
> too much television, and was too dependent on her adult
> children for social contact. In this particular case, the client

was trying to please her children and did not define herself as having a problem that required professional help. She was skeptical as to whether she belonged in therapy. "Yes," she stated, she was "a little depressed," but coming into therapy seemed too drastic to her. She did not return beyond two sessions.

In these situations, adequate time must be spent explaining the rationale and developing rapport with the client. Every effort must be made to elicit the client's perception of the problems and then show how the therapy program can address such issues. In instances where there is regular contact between the client and family members, it is usually helpful to inform the family (with the client's permission, of course) that the older adult is in a treatment program. Periodic contact with the family, especially during the follow-up phase, is also helpful. If the family is receptive, guidelines for family-client interactions can be extremely helpful.

In contrast, in cases where the client is "for" treatment and the family "against" it, family members may be suspicious of the behavioral approach or lack understanding of how it works (e.g., the connection between homework and treatment progress). It is important for the therapist to be sensitive to this; sometimes the situation can be improved.

The wife of one client sincerely wanted her husband to progress, but unwittingly was undermining this goal. She did not know that her husband had daily homework assignments which were essential to the treatment or that he was having difficulty developing a routine of activity tracking and other between-sessions work. The therapist learned that the couple did not work cooperatively to plan their activities. The wife typically wanted her husband to go out shopping after dinner or to go away for weekends, as they had done before he was depressed. The client began procrastinating on the tracking schedules and excused himself by saying that his wife wanted him to do something else that night.

One way to overcome this problem is to have the client explain and discuss the rationale for therapy with family members so the family will be more likely to understand and support the treatment— perhaps even encourage the client to persist at strategic times. The family can become an ally to provide incentive and positive reinforcement between sessions.

Other families may respond in a way that helps the client maintain his depression. Family members in the same household with the client often have adjusted to the depression and developed their own ways of perceiving and coping with it. If the depression has been long-standing or recurring, it has probably been incorporated into the family dynamics in complex ways.

> Some clients are so depressed that they stay in bed all day. One elderly gentleman had followed this pattern for years. His wife was so distraught at his behavior that she was extremely angry and became physically destructive toward him when he did this. Her behavior further depressed him and made him feel hopeless about his marriage.

When such maladaptive relationships exist at the same time as therapy efforts are attempting to bring about change, it may be wise to suggest separate therapy for other family members.

> In another situation, the client's wife was maintaining his depression by reminding him of many health problems which presumably prevented him from participating in a number of activities he had previously enjoyed (golf and other sports). Although the therapist had attempted to explain to the client's wife than an exercise program would be instituted only with medical consultation, the wife was extremely resentful of the therapist's intrusion into their family system. She perceived the therapist as a threat, and did everything she could to reinforce the client's helpless and hopeless feelings about himself. Not until the client decided, quite apart from the behavioral treatment itself, to obtain a divorce, did improvement occur.

A desire on the part of family members for a different *kind* of treatment for the client can pose problems, especially if they are actively or subtly campaigning for a change of therapist.

> One client wanted to try behavioral treatment, but her husband and children felt she should be hospitalized and given a series of shock treatments for presumably intractable depression. The client eventually dropped out of treatment and was hospitalized, despite the therapist's efforts to encourage the family to give behavioral therapy a trial.

Older depressed persons frequently seek treatment because of problems with their grown children, or with their own more elderly parents.

> A 55-year-old Mexican American client experienced extreme guilt as to how her adult children had turned out. She saw one of her daughters as a total failure in life. There was no way to ascertain the facts in the case; even had they been known, what had been done could not be undone. Establishing treatment goals was difficult. The therapist proceeded to investigate ways in which positive contact between mother and daughter could

be promoted. After thorough investigation, therapist and client agreed that no positive contact was possible at that point in time. Once visits and phone calls were stopped, the client's anxiety and depression lifted considerably. She began to focus on how she could assist in the raising of several grandchildren who were important to her and could give her positive feedback.

Finally, learning how to cope with multiple problems surrounding the needs of a considerably older parent can be a major treatment goal. The client may need to make some decisions about the parent's future (placement in a nursing home or other extended care facility), and in the process experience feelings of extreme guilt. Therapy must proceed slowly enough to permit the guilt feelings to be expressed during the same period that information is being gathered about facilities available, types of services offered, and the general milieu of each. Thus, when the placement is made, it will be the best possible decision under the circumstances. In these cases, considerable flexibility in the treatment program is advised, the modifications in the "standard approach" presented in this manual may be necessary. Homework assignments will need to be clearly focused on the issue at hand; creativity on the therapist's part is essential so that the presenting problem is in fact resolved by the end of treatment.

MEDICAL PROBLEMS

Because numerous medical problems (both chronic and acute) and physical handicaps (such as diminished vision and hearing) occur more frequently among older persons, it is important to understand the nature of these problems and to evaluate their potential impact on treatment. To avoid having sessions become an outlet for idle complaining, medical concerns should be discussed in terms of constructive ways of dealing with them. Some clients need to be guided away from repetitive discussion and preoccupation with physical complaints, yet it is important that they not be ignored completely.

The client must be encouraged to use the abilities which remain rather than focus on what has been lost.

A client with severe visual problems and associated pain wanted to spend the majority of each session explaining how her vision problem had affected the various aspects of her life since the preceding session. The therapist directed the client to take a problem solving approach; at the same time, he acknowledged and sympathized with the woman's handicap. The client was instructed to list those pleasant events she *could* engage in, using her Pleasant Events Schedule as a guide. Once the list was completed, much time was spent discussing how the frequency of these activities could be increased.

One of the effects of her vision problem was a loss of night vision, which resulted in her being unable to drive at night.

Since she enjoyed many social activities, she needed either to find daytime activities or to depend on husband or friends to provide nighttime transportation. She was directed to local colleges and senior centers for daytime activities, but the evenings were another issue. Before the vision problem developed, she had been extremely independent, and she now felt uncomfortable asking anyone for assistance. This pointed to the appropriateness of assertion training, which was useful in helping her (as it had many other clients) to deal with health care professionals as well as immediate family members. The training eventually enabled her to obtain more precise information about her vision and eye care, which in turn allowed for a more realistic appraisal of her condition.

A simple adjustment for clients with diminished vision is to provide large-print forms and reading handouts. Even with large print, however, completing written homework can be aversive when close work results in eye strain, and special attention should be devoted to minimizing this aversiveness. Methods found to be helpful include scheduling the homework to include breaks, helping the client set up self rewards for completing work, and providing special reinforcement during the therapy session.

Dealing with the anxiety surrounding visits to doctors' offices is a frequent problem for older persons, and this situation provides a good place to begin relaxation training. Older persons spend a great deal of time in doctors' offices.

An elderly female client became very nervous and irritable for several hours before each scheduled doctor's appointment, so that by the time she left home for the appointment, she would have often initiated an argument with her husband and be suffering from the effects of hyperventilation. When she had become familiar with the relaxation exercises, preparation for the visits was incorporated into the covert rehearsal portion of the relaxation sessions. She overcame her anxieties very rapidly and was able to arrive at the doctor's office feeling much more relaxed.

A number of medical illnesses, most notably cardiovascular disease and diabetes, may actually create depression in older adults. In these instances, consultation with the treating physician is absolutely essential to be sure that the depression is not physiological in origin. If, instead, depression stems from the client's inability to *adapt* to the illness, it may be responsive to behavioral therapy. Conversely, changes in the actual situation can have significant effects on treatment. In the following example, medical and psychological factors interacted in a negative way with a particular client.

> A 75-year-old male being treated fairly successfully with behavioral therapy had a history of ear troubles which included a persistent ringing in the ears. Eventually, he confided in his therapist, telling him he feared he had contracted syphilis during the time he served in World War II. A team of medical experts subsequently confirmed this diagnosis, and at that point the client became totally unreachable in terms of the behavioral approach. He was convinced his brain was rotting and that the future held nothing but a downhill course for him despite what he might do at present. He felt doomed, and became so severely depressed that he needed to be hospitalized and remained an inpatient for some time. During his inpatient medical workup, the earlier diagnosis was found less definitive.
>
> Instead of being relieved at the ambiguity of the situation, the client plummeted into an even deeper depression. He felt the medical profession could not be trusted, and that there was now even less hope for him because of the uncertainty under which he would have to live for the rest of his life. Eventually, he got some relief from his depression by moving out of the state and resuming relationships with adult sons from whom he had been estranged for several years.

Dealing with the medical problems common in the later years can be complex. The nature and extent of actual physical limitations should be carefully considered before designing behavioral treatment sessions and homework assignments. This is best done through regular consultation with the primary physician; then older adults can be treated effectively with behavioral methods even when medical problems are apparent. However, there will be a percentage of cases in which the severity of the medical condition will inhibit substantially any progress through behavioral therapy, and in such cases referral to a psychiatrist along with the institution of somatic kinds of treatment may be necessary.

FINANCIAL CONCERNS

Because income after retirement is usually substantially reduced, many clinics and mental health agencies serving the elderly use a sliding fee scale. We have found it advisable to establish some fee, even a minimal one, in order to legitimize therapy as important and worthwhile and to validate the client's ability to function as a normal member of society. The fee sets therapy in the context of being a service that is rendered rather than a friendly visit or "listening ear" approach. Yet the reality of the older person's economic situation must be considered in setting fees. The client's financial situation should be explored early, and whatever financial agreement is made should be very clear to all concerned.

Unfortunately, policies of the federal government, including Medicare, do not encourage reimbursement for psychological counseling with this age group. Thus, older individuals (except those with certain kinds of private insurance such as Blue Cross or Champus) will usually have to pay fees from their own resources. This may present a hardship for extended treatment, and for this reason the short term design of behavioral therapy has appeal to older individuals.

If clients resist paying anything for treatment, their expectations of the therapist and his role should be examined. Clients who refuse to pay any fee, or make a major issue of paying even when a sliding scale is used, tend to drop out very quickly. Given an honest appraisal of an individual's economic situation, payment of a fee for behavioral therapy rendered should be encouraged.

SUMMARY

Many treatment issues emerge when socioeconomic, cultural, family, medical, and financial factors inherent in the problems of older persons are considered. Therapists need to be sensitive to socioeconomic and cultural factors, and learn to operate within their limits. With regard to the role of the family, the rule of thumb is "Consult with family members in all cases where client interacts with them regularly, and elicit their cooperation if possible." If their cooperation cannot be achieved, efforts should concentrate on strengthening the client's resolve to change.

At the outset of therapy, family cooperation is impossible to predict. However, consulting with members and educating them as to what behavioral treatment consists of will usually increase the prospects of treatment success. In cases where the family clearly resists behavioral treatment, the client is unlikely to overcome the pressure, and an appropriate referral should be considered.

Medical and financial problems often cannot be changed. Therapists must find creative ways of working around them and try to change the client's attitude toward them.

II.

TECHNICAL

ISSUES

4 Broad Technical Issues for the Therapist

Several general issues frequently arise for the therapist doing behavioral treatment with older persons: (1) protocol in the structure of therapy and client-therapist relationship, (2) attitudes of client and therapist which may interfere with the course of treatment, (3) counter-transference reactions, and (4) premature termination. These issues should be considered before commencing treatment, as they may arise early in problematic form if not anticipated and prepared for.

PROTOCOL

Repetition of Rationale and Instructions

In the first treatment session, considerable time will be devoted to an explanation of the rationale for behavioral therapy. Some commitment will be obtained from the client to cooperate with this approach, yet after the first few sessions, the client may seem to be unable to utilize the rationale in specific situations (may have forgotten; may consider it inapplicable to the circumstances). While this may be frustrating to the therapist and suggest resistance to treatment, a more adaptive explanation is that the older individual requires more *time* to learn and put into practice new ideas than a younger person (Botwinick, 1978). Older persons also need assistance to translate ideas into concrete, everyday realities specific to their situations. Thus, the therapist needs to be creative, flexible, and persistent when presenting and re-presenting material. He should patiently and frequently present examples of the treatment rationale which are relevant for the individual client.

Multimodal presentation of information is very useful in this regard. For example, the therapist should (1) have the client rephrase ideas; (2) role play so the client can practice the skill and the therapist supply feedback; and (3) use blackboards, audio-visuals, and graphic presentations to reinforce points.

State-dependent learning has also been found to contribute to the need for repetition in behavioral therapy. A client who understands and uses a skill in a treatment session may not, when depressed outside the treatment hour, see how the skill applies to that situation. The client will need to relearn the skill in the everyday life situation. Aids that can assist in this transfer of learning need to be developed for each client. It is also helpful for the client to understand how state-dependent learning operates so he can be forewarned and not become overly discouraged when it happens.

Limiting the Advocacy Role

Often therapists beginning work with older adults feel they should take an advocacy role and thereby facilitate the client's access to needed information or services. Yet it is important to ask how much should be done "for" the client. Guidelines will need to be developed by the therapist to maintain a desirable balance; he needs to provide appropriate assistance, yet encourage the client to do things on his own. In this situation, separating a task into small progressive steps that can be accomplished one at a time is very helpful.

> If a call needs to be placed to a social agency to arrange for Meals On Wheels, the client could be assigned the task of looking up the phone number or securing it from Information. In a treatment session, he could review the salient point and practice making the call (perhaps even make it then).

Although this approach is time consuming (the therapist could secure the information more quickly), the client can learn a great deal about developing a skill that can be used in other situations.

Constructive Use of Therapy Time

A troublesome issue in treatment is misuse of time by the client. For example, it is not unusual for older clients to talk at great length and in great detail about all sorts of events which have transpired.

While this can provide helpful information for treatment planning, it can also lead to discussion of essentially irrelevant material during precious therapy time. When such detailed explanations have little relevance to the topic being discussed, they waste time and should be terminated.

> To terminate a conversation, it is appropriate for the therapist
> to politely interrupt and direct the client to more relevant
> material: "I can surely understand how these things can upset
> you, but I think what you really need to focus on is . . ."

Most clients understand the therapist's intentions and respond accordingly. Occasionally, they do not respond and continue to talk. In such cases it may be necessary for the therapist to assert himself by speaking markedly louder than the client to effect the change in topic. In extreme cases other techniques may be employed: (1) thought-stopping (the therapist calls out "Stop," and teaches the client how to stop himself; (2) physically standing above client while loudly requesting the change in conversation topic.

The most effective way to limit conversation is to create an agenda. The therapist begins the session by asking whether there is anything in particular the client wishes to discuss, and if so, time is allotted either at the beginning or end of the session (the end is preferred; less clock time is available, which helps control time spent on non-central issues).

In cases where a client's excessive or tangential conversation could be interpreted as a struggle with the therapist for control of the session, it should be made clear that the therapist has the principal responsibility for planning and directing treatment. Though the client is an integral part of the planning process and must agree with what is to be covered in each session, it is the therapist's responsibility to be sure an agenda is established and followed at each meeting.

Homework

Because homework is an integral part of this therapy, it is necessary to stress with the client the importance of completing all homework assignments in order to gain the greatest benefit from therapy. The rationale for assignment and completion of homework should be carefully explained, emphasizing that the homework exercises are necessary for learning new skills, providing a system for self-monitoring behaviors and mood, and evaluating progress.

The details of each assignment must be carefully explained and feedback elicited to be sure client understands the homework; an example should be examined with the client whenever possible. The client should write out the assignment for each session in his notebook; this will be a reminder to complete the homework. The therapist also should keep a record of each assignment.

If a client fails to complete the homework, time must be spent assessing the reasons for the failure. The assignment may have been too complex, and should be broken into smaller segments in the future. The client may not have understood the purpose of the assignment; in that case, make a clear connection between the task and the skill to be learned. Complaints that the assignment was too time-consuming can be countered by pointing out that the purpose of homework is to facilitate learning skills that can be used after therapy has been terminated, and this takes practice.

The therapist can reinforce the client's efforts to complete assignments by (1) encouraging him to confront whatever specific difficulties are being experienced, (2) helping him to develop self-rewards for completion, and (3) *always* reviewing the completed homework early in each session to show its relevance to therapy progress. If necessary, the client should be helped to set a definite, scheduled time each day for completing assignments.

In addition to homework designed to develop skills, more general reading or writing assignments may be effective learning tools for certain clients. These could include summaries of important points gleaned during a session or from readings, or expansion of issues insufficiently covered during a session (pinpointing problem situations; listing items the client wishes to include in the next agenda). This material, when included in the client's notebook, will be useful after termination of therapy.

Use of a "fantasy session" is also helpful to stimulate motivation when sessions are spaced out for a week or longer. Clients frequently lose momentum three to four days after a weekly session, and homework compliance then drops noticeably. An effective way to deal with this problem is to assign specific tasks for the client to accomplish on his own on a day between sessions when motivation needs to be reinforced. These tasks could be going over notes, completing homework for that day, and noting any issues to be discussed in the coming session; they should be approached as though they were part of a clinic session.

Progress will be slowed if the client gets into the habit of recording homework material late, days after the assignment was carried out. This leads to inaccuracy and conclusions that can be misleading. Instead, the client should be encouraged to make consistent use of the notebook to record homework *every day*. If the client has not had time to complete this work prior to each session, part of the actual session time should be devoted to this task. This emphasizes the importance of regular recording, and usually does not have to be done more than once.

Older depressed individuals may complete the "letter," but not the "spirit" of the assignment. They may report the completion of a homework task and record it in the notebook, but be basically inaccurate in their written and verbal account—yet they may or may not be aware of this inaccuracy. For example:

> An older male client reports success in learning to relax, yet when asked to demonstrate his relaxation technique in the session, he yells, with his arms waving and sitting on the edge of his chair, "I am relaxed, I am very relaxed; can't you see that? I don't need to show you how relaxed I am."

Obviously, there is a problem. By having clients demonstrate specific skills on which they have been working, the therapist can encourage reports consistent with actual behavior and promote adaptive changes.

In short, homework is the very heart of behavioral therapy. Rather than being a mechanical procedure, homework provides the client with opportunities to put into practice what he has learned. Clients who refuse to do homework despite efforts to simplify it and encourage compliance are poor prognostic risks. Homework is so integral to behavioral treatment that clients should be told directly that those who do not actively participate in the assignments are unlikely to benefit from the therapy.

Setting Professional Limits

Therapists may be approached with social or recreational offers from older clients who may see this as a way to increase activities and build social skills, particularly friendship. While recognizing the ethical risks, the therapist may be more vulnerable to stretching the limits with older clients who are often lonely, inactive, and bored. However, such activities are ultimately self-defeating.

The aims of behavioral treatment are (1) to develop a generic set of skills for coping with depression and (2) to promote autonomy rather than dependence. Accordingly, offers of gifts or social or recreational activities should be declined. (The reasons for this are based on the specific aims of treatment as well as clients' motivations and expectations for therapy.) In this way misconceptions can be corrected, seeing therapy as primarily palliative can be avoided, and anxiety about the short term of therapy (which may underly social offers) can be resolved. Feelings of rejection may also diminish when therapy is framed in a learning context which makes the need for professional limits apparent. Nevertheless, it is prudent to check out the client's reaction (and try to reduce any discomfort) whenever limits need to be explicitly established.

ATTITUDES OF CLIENT AND THERAPIST

Client Attitudes

Clients sometimes feel they are "set in their ways," and that although they may be able to change some behaviors through therapy, so many will remain that therapy will make minimal difference. This can be handled by reframing the task from "changing" to "learning." Does the client think he is too old to *learn* anything new? Has anything specific been learned recently? If so, then additional new learning can occur, and if not, he can be encouraged to assume an experimental attitude and give this approach a try. If in fact no new learning seems to occur in two to four weeks of therapy, then a referral should be considered to a less demanding type of treatment.

"You're too young to help me." Doubts about the competence of therapists one or two generations younger than the clients must be treated in a straightforward manner, with no defensiveness. These doubts are often based on the client's assumption that a person must experience the same event to fully understand it. This attitude can be challenged by the therapist through pointing out that he can learn from the client's account and has been through similar experiences which have yielded insights as to how depression can come about. Soliciting the client's help in understanding an experience will enhance the collaborative relationship necessary for change. Pointing to the fact that physicians need not experience appendicitis to be able to treat it, that social workers need not be poor and victimized to help clients, and that nurses do not have to experience an illness to provide proper care for patients will help to deal with this problem.

"If only X would change, I wouldn't be depressed." Clients often bring a hidden agenda to therapy, believing that removing X problem or changing Y person will automatically cause the depression to lift. This condition is often found where there is significant family conflict or other environmental stress.

> Situations such as marital separation, a difficult spouse or sibling, or illness lead the client to think the depression is caused by the situation and therefore cannot change unless the person or situation changes first. This position is untenable for behavioral therapy, because such elements are beyond the client's control and usually are not the crux of the depression anyway.

The therapist needs to skillfully translate these presenting concerns into a framework amenable to behavioral treatment (e.g., what can the client work on to reduce his discomfort in this situation). This can be accomplished by linking the specific concern with the treatment rationale and involving the client in specifying behaviors that can in fact be changed. Once the locus of responsibility has shifted (from X or Y to the client), reduction in depression will usually follow.

"THESE TECHNIQUES AREN'T REALLY APPLICABLE TO ME"

Clients may be unwilling to learn certain techniques because they feel the methods do not apply to their needs. At times, the client is right in his perception (for example, he may already have found a relaxation technique which is successful, and resists learning the technique suggested in this manual). However, at other times clients are unwilling to learn specific behavioral skills due to lack of a clear understanding of the treatment rationale and how skill training relates to their everyday problems. A careful review of the relationship between skill training and improvement usually helps considerably.

Sometimes older clients are not working in treatment because of poor choices of practice situations by therapists. For example, a relatively isolated older person may need to approach the problem of increasing social interactions *slowly*. To do this, the social skill should be broken down into component parts, and they should be practiced one at a time before being integrated into the whole. This may require a number of sessions in order to avoid pressuring the client for too much change too quickly. In an effort to speed up progress, easy situations likely to guarantee success may be bypassed, thus yielding frustration for both therapist and client. Also, as noted earlier, sociocultural factors may inhibit an older person from adopting currently popular behavioral interventions such as assertiveness training and sexual modification programs. The therapist's task is to creatively modify techniques to suit each client's needs, skill level, and cultural background.

Nevertheless, instances remain where a client will not utilize a technique even when appropriate. Rather than pursue the issue, the therapist should back off and identify another problem area which can be more easily treated, for example:

> A recovered alcoholic client, a female who was being treated with behavioral therapy, refused to resume attendance at AA meetings even though she had been carefully, step by step, working toward this goal and knew it was important to

maintain her sobriety. Despite the fact that she had investigated several AA groups in her area and knew they had a fair representation of older women in their membership, she was unable to take the final step—to get herself to an AA meeting.

The therapist decided that a suitable alternative would be to encourage the client to call other AA members by phone to get support; the client found numerous excuses not to pursue even that alternative. The issue was dropped, and therapy changed focus to some of the women's other problems. What came to light was an extremely negative self-image, and shame at having been an alcoholic for a number of years. She felt that everyone she met would know about it and therefore would not wish to associate with her.

The therapist decided that working on these negative self statements would be more profitable to the client, and the treatment plan was changed to focus on modification of negative self talk, which proved successful.

The client may find considerable benefit from treatment even if behaviors and techniques initially chosen for focus are not used following the original plan. Openness and flexibility on the part of the therapist are valuable assets.

Therapist Attitudes

The therapist needs to examine his own attitudes, especially at the outset of clinical practice. They may be negative, reflecting sociocultural stereotypes about aging to which we have all been exposed. Older people *are* different from younger persons in a number of respects. Some of these differences make responsiveness to behavioral therapy a difficult task for the older individual; for example, increased cautiousness and decreased risk-taking characterize the behavior of many elders (Kogan & Wallach, 1964). Still, this does not mean that old persons cannot change; positive attitudes on this and other stereotypes through creative, persistent, flexible, and focused therapy can set the climate for change.

The natural deference young therapists may display toward older people ("respect your elders") could affect the need to be directive in treatment. The therapist will need to interrupt during sessions to keep the client on track; consequently, he needs to feel comfortable about interrupting and refocusing to avoid losing valuable therapy time (older people do seem to go off on tangents at times). By structuring interruptions into the session at its outset (explaining that interruptions will probably be necessary to maintain focus on the mutually-decided agenda), the meeting's task-oriented goal can be strengthened.

Therapists accustomed to working with younger individuals may find that progress with older persons is slower (clients may have difficulty doing behavioral homework assignments, for example). The early stages of treatment can be frustrating, yet by staying with the issue persistently, "blocks" can be resolved; patience and toleration of frustration are attitudes to be cultivated by therapists who work with older depressed individuals.

COUNTERTRANSFERENCE REACTIONS

The term "countertransference" as used here means accepting a client's negative evaluation of his capacity for change (or "buying into" his depressogenic belief system). Countertransference problems are frequent in behavioral treatment of older persons.

> An individual who is experiencing severe loss of visual acuity may find it impossible to do a number of things, such as driving a car or reading average print.

The therapist who becomes as discouraged as the client obviously cannot assist him to learn new skills. The therapist should focus on how the client can adapt in more functional ways to the disabling condition rather than on the discouragement or providing sympathy. For example, in the case of visual problems, emphasis should be placed on the kinds of compensatory devices available, the programs designed to assist people who are partially sighted, and on encouraging any and all activities the individual can still enjoy.

Therapists of any theoretical persuasion can be ineffective when client issues "hit close to home." If a client is concerned about waning sexuality and this is a projected future concern of the therapist, it may be difficult to encourage the usual behavioral management programs for increasing sexual activity: To be aware of the possibility of such a factor occurring is helpful in order to maintain perspective. Health decline is another sensitive area for therapists. They may see the same kinds of declines in their family members, or fear similar declines in themselves. An optimal way to resolve this dilemma is to accept the fact that X negative event has occurred and at the same time maintain a behavioral optimism that there are still aspects of life than can be pleasant and satisfying for the client.

PREMATURE TERMINATION

Premature termination is a problem in all modes of psychotherapy. In a survey of research on continuation in psychotherapy, Garfield and Bergin (1978) have reported that fully one-half of clients accepted into treatment dropped out before the eighth session. For our time-limited behavioral therapy, the figure is somewhat lower. Yet even low rates of premature termination represent wasted manpower and in some cases failure of the therapy. It is therefore worthwhile to review some of the apparent reasons for early drop-out from therapy and present some possible solutions.

The reasons most often given by clients for dropping out of therapy are related to logistical problems: scheduling difficulties, lack of transportation, or a shortage of money. With older clients, these issues are often realistic. While older clients may have ample free time to schedule therapy, they may strongly object to appointments which require going out at night or during hours of the day when traffic is heavy and buses are crowded with school-age riders.

Inadequate transportation is probably the major logistical obstacle for older clients. A relative who was eager to act as chauffeur for the initial session may be unwilling or unable to maintain this commitment over weeks or months. In such cases, the therapist should provide direct assistance in finding alternative transportation whenever possible.

To minimize the incidence of drop-out due to logistic problems, the therapist needs to play an active problem-solving role. For example, consider the following telephone conversation which took place after the fourth session of treatment:

Client: Dr. S., I won't be able to come to your office any more. I'm sorry if this inconveniences you; I called as soon as I found out so you could schedule some-one else in my place.

Therapist: *What's the problem?*

Client: My son found a new job, so he can't drive me any more.

Therapist: *Is there anyone else who could drive you?*

Client: Oh, no; I wouldn't ask anyone to drive me some place every week.

Therapist: *Is there anyone who has ever offered to drive you some place if you needed a ride?*

Client: Well—the lady next door, but I couldn't ask her to drive me and then wait for an hour every week.

Therapist: *O.K. Anyone else?*

Client: My daughter-in-law drives me to the doctor.

Therapist: *Anyone else?*

Client: Just my son. But he'll be working every day 9 to 5, and I wouldn't ask him to take me out at night.

Therapist: *What if he just picked you up from my office on his way home?*

Client: But we meet so much earlier than that.

Therapist: *Would it be possible for you to change the session time to 4 p.m.?*

Client: Yes.

Therapist: *During our first session, you said you could call a cab if your son occasionally was not able to bring you. Do you think sometimes you could take a cab, and then have your son pick you up?*

Client: That would be too expensive every week.

Therapist: *But could you do it sometimes? Maybe once a month?*

Client: Yes, I guess so.

Therapist: *And what about your daughter-in-law? Do you think she'd mind driving you to my office a couple of times during the next month?*

Client: I don't know. I guess I could ask her.

Therapist: *And what about that neighbor? Do you think she could drive you here once or twice a month?*

Thus, although the client was reluctant to inconvenience anyone, a solution to a very real problem was available, and required only minimal assistance from three separate individuals. Arranging the final transportation schedule involved the therapist making two additional phone calls—a negligible investment in light of the benefit this client received from therapy.

At times logistical problems are used to mask the real reasons for early termination. This becomes apparent when no problem-solving attempts are acceptable to the client. In such cases, it is important for the therapist to probe to uncover the real reason or reasons for the client's withdrawal.

After transportation, the next most common reason for dropping out relates to problems completing homework. Clients sometimes resent being asked to carry out the assignments; this is particularly true of "professional clients" (individuals who have spent many years in psychotherapy of one form or another). Homework represents to them a radical departure from their psychotherapy expectations, and one which consequently may threaten their sense of control or undermine their confidence in the treatment modality. Homework is also a problem for clients who (for whatever reasons) never successfully complete their assignments. This contributes to feelings of frustration and inadequacy, and inevitably damages the rapport between therapist and client.

If the client decides to drop out of treatment because of homework-related problems, the therapist can take several steps to forestall termination:

1. Negotiate a trial extension of therapy.
2. Re-explain the purpose and value of homework.
3. Express understanding of the difficulties involved in completing homework, especially if the problem centers around completion.
4. Make some compromise if the client feels the work load is too heavy.
5. Help the client to schedule time to work on the assignments.
6. Make an assignment which has a high probability of success, then provide ample reinforcement to the client upon successful completion.
7. Schedule a phone call during the week to check client's progress; if problems are being experienced, a new plan can be formulated at this time.

If these attempts to avoid termination are unsuccessful, it may be that the client should go elsewhere for treatment. The primary issue is: "At what point must this tretment be discontinued?" There is no easy answer. Each situation will be different, and because of the myriad and unavoidable factors mentioned earlier, there will be a percentage of drop-outs.

On the other hand, the therapist has the prerogative of terminating treatment if sessions do not seem beneficial. Clients who persist in undermining treatment and frustrating therapist efforts may need to have sessions terminated to avoid reinforcing their idea that, despite the best efforts of everyone, they cannot change. Useful in these circumstances is a comparison of depression levels before treatment and at the point they are considering dropping out; frequently there have been changes, and this will help discourage premature termination. When this also fails to increase commitment, termination should be accepted, and the therapist should study the case to seek any factors that might have altered the outcome. This review may prove fruitful in some cases, yet in others may shed no new light since the client may have been unconvinced from the outset that behavioral treatment was right for him.

To repeat, clients who comply with treatment expectations, sincerely complete homework assignments, and make whatever efforts are needed to attend sessions are those who are most likely to perceive behavioral therapy as beneficial to them. These clients are giving behavioral treatment a fair try; others may have been shopping around for some time for the "right" treatment, and flee rapidly to other professionals when faced with the reality of *self*-change emphasized in behavioral therapy.

By carefully documenting the reasons for premature termination in a number of cases treated, information useful in work with future clients can be uncovered. It has been the policy of the Andrus Center therapists to routinely contact drop-out clients approximately three to six months after termination and request an additional interview at that time. Such meetings usually provide greater clarity as to the reasons for the client's behavior. By that time the client has been able to put behavioral therapy into some kind of perspective and can discuss it in depth. The information secured has proved useful for refining the approach for subsequent clients.

SUMMARY

Many technical problems can be anticipated to occur with great regularity in treating older adults. The therapist must pay attention to a number of protocol items.

Frequent repetition of rationale and instructions will help to keep this important material fresh in the minds of clients. The advocacy role should be avoided as much as possible. The clinician should be alert to any need for increased structuring of therapy time. He should also be prepared to make extra effort in seeing that homework assignments are appropriate, feasible, and are completed on time. Attitudes of both client and therapist are important determinants of therapy outcome. These need to be monitored and addressed as treatment proceeds. On the client's part, common themes include: "I'm too old to change"; "You're too young to help me"; "These techniques aren't really appropriate for me." Therapists must be careful that they do not let negative stereotypes of the elderly influence their impressions of the client. Countertransference issues, for example, frequently occur and can block the therapy process. Finally, a serious problem than embodies many of these issues is premature termination. All of these technical problems must be dealt with in order for therapy to progress smoothly.

Assessing Symptoms and Measuring Change 5

This chapter will present in detail information needed to diagnose depression, measure baseline behaviors, and assess change. Without careful attention to these crucial issues, it is impossible to determine the effectiveness of behavioral treatment. This comprehensive presentation has been provided to serve the large audience for whom the manual is intended.

DIAGNOSTIC ISSUES

As noted earlier, assessment of depression in older persons is a complex matter, and therefore suggestions based on clinical and research experience with this problem at U.S.C. can provide helpful guidelines for proceeding. Still, the state of the art is rapidly changing, and practitioners should not regard these findings as "the last word" on diagnosis; they should also keep abreast of the emerging literature in this regard. References to primary work have been provided whenever possible so that clinicians can become familiar with the issues and perhaps modify the suggestions presented to best meet needs in particular clinical settings.

Comprehensive Assessment: The Structured Interview

In clinical research settings where appropriate classification is a major concern, use of a structured interview developed specifically to provide a reliable index of depressive syndrome, the Schedule for Affective Disorders and Schizophrenia (SADS) developed by researchers at the New York State Psychiatric Institute (Endicott & Spitzer, 1978), is recommended.[1] The SADS typically requires 1½ hours to administer, and should be used only by clinicians trained to make the required clinical judgments.[2] Information obtained through administering the SADS is used to establish diagnoses according to specific criteria found in the Research Diagnostic Criteria manual (RDC) also published by this group. Development and use of the RDC are discussed in a paper by Spitzer, Endicott, and Robins (1978).

There has been some question as to the appropriateness for the elderly of the SADS/RDC system, which was originally developed and used primarily with depressed individuals under the age of 60. A recently completed U.S.C./University of Oregon collaborative study of the diagnostic utility of this approach with older adults has shown encouraging results (Dessonville, Gallagher, Thompson, & Finnell, 1980). The SADS/RDC approach has been found reliable with elderly clients in that symptoms used to establish a "major depressive disorder" diagnosis appeared significantly less frequently in a nondepressed elderly community sample than in the elderly group diagnosed as depressed. The depressed clients reported much greater affective distress, somatic complaints, and cognitive complaints than their non-depressed counterparts (matched for age and health status).

In the U.S.C./University of Oregon study, the SADS/RDC techniques were supplemented with several other measures to evaluate whether specific symptoms were part of the depressive syndrome or could be attributed to other causes. For example, somatic symptoms such as sleep and appetite disturbances may often reflect an illness other than depression. For this reason, it is necessary to evaluate health status independently. Medication usage should also be evaluated, as a number of medications (e.g., the antihypertensives) used by older persons are known to increase the probability of depressive symptoms. Salzman and Shader (1979) have provided an excellent comprehensive review of specific illnesses and medications implicated in the origin of depression.

Several methods can be helpful in determining the relative contribution of physical health status and current medication usage to the older client's presenting symptoms. Clients could complete a checklist of illnesses and medicines such as that developed by Raskin and Crook (1978)[3] before the SADS interview so that this supplementary information is available to the interviewer and can be used to clarify responses. Physicians could determine the relevant information through physical examinations or review of existing medical records. The least costly and time-consuming approach is to ask the client to rate his perceived physical health status on a simple four-point scale (1=excellent, 2=good, 3=fair, 4=poor). This appears to be a reliable method for screening purposes, as this self-perception correlates well with physician's health ratings (LaRue, Bank, Jarvik, & Hetland, 1979). Ratings of "fair" or "poor" should be followed up with direct questions as to the reasons for the rating; responses should be recorded to assist in interpretation of questions about somatic symptoms on the SADS.

In addition to such physical health information, an independent measure of cognitive functioning should also be obtained. Many older persons complain of diminished cognitive abilities (memory problems, poor concentration, or difficulty with new learning). These complaints may reflect early stages of dementia or other neurological disturbance which would contraindicate use of behavioral treatment. More typically, however, they are symptoms of depression in older persons.

Because determining the origin of these cognitive symptoms is difficult, neurological evaluation may be necessary. However, a brief cognitive screening measure with established reliability for this age group may effectively avoid this expensive kind of test. The Mini Mental State Examination (Folstein, Folstein, & McHugh, 1975) is especially good because it taps various aspects of cognitive functioning, hence qualitative as well as quantitative results can be analyzed. Other useful measures of mental status have been developed by Pfeiffer (1975) and Kahn, Goldfarb, Pollack, & Peck (1960).

To summarize, the SADS/RDC approach supplemented by measures of physical health, medication use, and cognitive functioning is strongly recommended where accuracy of diagnosis is critical. This kind of systematic evaluation insures minimum error and justifies the time invested.

Alternative Approaches

Less expensive and time-consuming methods may be feasible in mental health settings where thorough assessments (as described above) are not possible due to time constraints. Several possibilities can be suggested.

Self-report measures. First, there are a number of self-report scales used by practitioners and mental health agencies to determine whether depression is the client's primary problem. Among these are multidimensional measures such as the MMPI (Hathaway & McKinley, 1943) or the Hopkins Symptom Checklist (HSCL) (Derogatis, Lipman, & Covi, 1973) and/or their short forms. These scales were not originally normed on elderly samples, and thus scores obtained can be difficult to interpret (see Harmatz & Shader, 1975, for an example of how response set bias affects the scores of older adults on the MMPI depression scale). Other measures such as the Zung Self-Rating Depression Scale (SDS; Zung, 1965) and the Beck Depression Inventory (BDI; Beck, Ward, Mendelson, Mock, & Erbaugh, 1961), were also developed primarily from work with younger clients.

Recent research indicates that these last two measures can, nevertheless, be quite useful with older persons (McGarvey, Gallagher, & Thompson, in press; Gallagher & Nies, 1981). Their reliability is adequate for certain purposes, and they appear to be valid measures of depression in the old. Scores on the SDS and BDI are usually totaled and then evaluated in terms of being above or below a specific cut-off. Zung (1967) has found that a cut-off score of 58 or greater on the SDS with older persons is a clinically relevant index of depression. This score represents one standard deviation above the mean score obtained with a fairly large sample of non-depressed community-residing elderly. The standard cut-off of 17 or greater on the BDI for a "moderate" level of depression has been found to correctly classify 91 percent of a sample of depressed elderly assessed by SADS/RDC methods (Gallagher, Stone, & Thompson, 1981). Still, a self-report measure correctly normed to persons over 60 needs to be developed so that greater confidence can be placed in this method of assessment.

Brief clinical interviews. A second approach to diagnosis is to conduct a semi-structured interview with the client. The interview should cover major symptom areas which are part of the clinical syndrome of depression.

There are two possible techniques. One is to use the Hamilton Rating Scale (HRS; Hamilton, 1960, 1967) which taps many aspects of depression (affective distress, guilt, pessimism, various somatic complaints, and loss of interest in daily activities). It contains the areas to be explored and rated, but guidelines for how to ask questions are minimial; also, a large number of its items are on somatic symptoms (9 out of 17). Considering interviewer variability in asking questions and the already-mentioned difficulty of assessing whether somatic symptoms truly reflect depression in the old, it can be hard to obtain reliable information from the HRS as it now stands. To improve its usefulness with elderly clients, a series of "probes" have been constructed for use with the somatic questions.[4] Further research is needed to determine whether the standard cut-off score of 14 or greater (traditionally the criterion for "moderate" depression with the HRS) is appropriate for the elderly.

The second possibility for structuring the diagnostic interview, and one which may be preferable to the modified Hamilton approach when time permits, is to ask about the symptom cluster defined by Feighner and colleagues (Feighner, Robins, & Guze, 1972). The Feighner criteria actually form the basis for both the RDC and current DSM III diagnostic categories. This kind of interview includes five areas:

1. **How long has the current episode lasted?** A duration of two weeks or greater usually rules out clients with only the transitory symptoms common in the upper age ranges.

2. **What has been the main feeling state during that time?** Clear presence of dysphoria as the predominant mood is necessary. Older persons often do not label their "down" feelings as depression, but feelings of sadness, pessimism, helplessness, and other euphemisms for depression suffice.

3. **What kinds of distress has the person experienced?** Specific inquiry should be made into the following: ideas of suicide (or actual suicidal behavior), increased or decreased appetite, increased or decreased need for sleep, loss of energy, fatigability or tiredness, psychomotor agitation or retardation, loss of interest or pleasure in usual activities including social contact or sex, feelings of self-reproach or excessive guilt, and complaints or evidence of diminished ability to think or concentrate such as slowed thinking or indecisiveness. The presence of four or more of the above-mentioned symptoms means a clinical problem is present. If the person has only one or two of these symptoms, a minor depression may be present.

4. **What has been the impact of this depressive state on the person's day-to-day functioning?** Ask about impairment in social roles (poor work functioning or inability to carry out family responsibilities), whether referred by someone for mental health treatment during the dysphoric period, whether medication has been taken to relieve the condition, or whether help has been sought from any source because of the current problem. Any one of these behavioral manifestations suggests a clinical level of distress.

5. **Can other significant problems (health problems, neurological problems, or other types of psychopathology such as a bipolar affective illness, current alcoholism, or residual schizophrenia) be ruled out as likely causes of the observed symptoms?**

The information obtained from the elderly client concerning these five areas must be sifted to determine whether the majority of areas covered yield positive findings. If the symptoms in the depressive cluster (No. 3 above) predominate and physical health problems, medication usage, or dementia-type processes can be ruled out, then the primary problem can be defined as affective in nature, and depression should be an accurate diagnosis.

How Diagnosis May Relate to Treatment

The importance of arriving at diagnosis carefully and systematically cannot be overemphasized, because this approach leads to appropriate treatment planning. Experience in work with the elderly indicates that those with unipolar depression are able to benefit substantially from psychosocial treatment which focuses on learning coping skills and improving the client's sense of self-efficacy (Gallagher, in press; Brown & Lewinsohn, 1980; Zarit, 1980). However, psychosocial approaches have not been evaluated to any great extent for their effectiveness with other kinds of psychiatric problems in the elderly such as bipolar affective illness, early stage dementia, or severe anxiety reactions. While there is reason to think they may in fact be appropriate interventions (cf. Knight, 1979), controlled studies are sorely needed.

Behavioral therapy is one of several psychosocial approaches; others include cognitive therapy (Beck, Rush, Shaw, & Emery, 1979), interpersonal therapy (Klerman, Rounsaville, & Chevron, 1979), and short term psychodynamically-oriented therapy (Wolberg, 1965). The decision to use behavioral treatment rather than another modality should be based on consideration of several factors: the client's motivation to participate in an active problem-solving treatment program, the therapist's commitment to social learning theory as a plausible way to explain the origin and maintenance of depression, and the presence of specific behavioral excesses or deficits that could become targets for intervention (see Kanfer & Saslow, 1969, for a fuller discussion of this latter point).

At present there are no hard and fast guidelines to help the clinician determine which older clients might benefit from behavioral therapy or when to select the behavioral approach over others in the clinician's repertoire. In general, good candidates are those who have few pleasant events and many unpleasant events in their daily lives. To assess the relative frequency of these kinds of events requires going a step beyond diagnosis to obtain an accurate picture of the client's daily life. It may or may not be practical to do this before treatment plans are formulated and assignment to a therapist is made. Typically, clients are assigned prior to a detailed behavioral work-up, and it is left to the therapist to determine the appropriate intervention strategy.

TARGETING BEHAVIORS FOR CHANGE

Several specific measures have proved essential in order to appropriately implement behavioral therapy. Five of these—Pleasant and Unpleasant Events Schedules, Pleasant and Unpleas-and Events Tracking Sheets, Mood Rating Form, behavioral graphing, and Relaxation Log Form—will be described next with recommendations for their use. Examples of these forms appear in the Appendix.

Pleasant and Unpleasant Events Schedules

During the first session, the client is asked to rate the 66 PES items as to pleasantness and frequency of occurrence and the 64 UES items as to aversiveness and frequency of occurrence. Ratings are on a 3-point scale.

Frequency dimension

0 = This has not happened in the past 30 days.
1 = This has happened a few times (1-6) in the past 30 days.
2 = This has happened often (7 times or more) in the past 30 days.

Pleasantness dimension

0 = This was not pleasant.
1 = This was somewhat pleasant.
2 = This was very pleasant.

Unpleasantness dimension

0 = This was not unpleasant.
1 = This was somewhat unpleasant.
2 = This was very unpleasant.

Completing the PES and the UES usually takes about 45 minutes. To help the client do this carefully and accurately it is important to explain the purpose of this procedure and how identification of potential and current reinforcers is the first step in treatment. The therapist should complete the first few items *with the client* to insure understanding of both the purpose and method of completing these forms. It may be necessary to help the client think of specific examples of items so responses accurately reflect his usual activities. When the client seems to understand how to complete both schedules, it is advisable to leave the room and then return periodically to check on progress, answer any questions, and provide positive feedback.

Some items may trigger thoughts or feelings which the client wishes to discuss with the therapist. The therapist should convey understanding and concern, yet see that the client does not deviate significantly from the task of completing the forms. The therapist might reframe the situation described by the client as a specific example for an item, then comment that several other items might also relate personally to some of the problems the client has been experiencing.

In general, it is both appropriate and profitable to use the PES and UES to generate discussion of specific problems. However, on the day of initial assessment when the client is required to complete both lists, too much discussion can delay the beginning of actual treatment.

Pleasant and Unpleasant Events Tracking Sheets

Between Session 1 and 2, individualized tracking sheets of 30 to 40 items must be created by the therapist for both pleasant and unpleasant events. Items on these personalized lists are to be determined by calculating directly on the PES and UES forms the cross-product for each event: score for frequency multiplied by the score for enjoyability (or aversiveness). For example, if "going to lunch" is circled 1 for frequency and 1 for enjoyment, the cross product is 1.

Events with the highest cross-products on the two scales are selected from this sequential criteria list until 30 to 40 items have been chosen from each:

Cross product = 4
Cross product = 2
Cross product = 1

Use of this hierarchical model leads to selection of the most meaningful events in each client's current environment.

Individualized Tracking Sheets are then set up for a period of seven days' monitoring by typing the items chosen on either the Pleasant Events or Unpleasant Events Tracking Sheet as appropriate. The client is to indicate each day whether each specific pleasant or unpleasant event occurred by checking the relevant box.

Presenting Tracking Sheets to the client. In Session 2, these Tracking Sheets are presented to the client with an explanation of how each set of items was obtained. The therapist should read every item with the client and encourage him to personalize each item with examples from his experience. It is also necessary to teach the client how to complete the Tracking Sheets at home, emphasizing the importance of *daily* tracking to the success of treatment.

Problems may arise at this point regarding content of items, attitudes toward assignment of daily tracking, or expressed doubts as to relevance of the approach. Regarding content, terms should be as individualized and concretized as possible for each client, hence no two persons' lists are ever exactly alike. Issues of compliance and treatment appropriateness need to be confronted directly; for example, it can be stated that without daily monitoring of pleasant and unpleasant activities, there will not be sufficient information for treatment to proceed. Clients who complain that this is not the right treatment for them should be encouraged to try it for two or three weeks; usually the Tracking Sheets and daily monitoring will make more sense by then and change will have begun to occur.

Content of Tracking Sheets. Items should be used in two ways. First, daily totals are generated to index the frequency of positive and negative; these are later plotted against mood fluctuations on the graphs (see below). Second, inspection of individual items provides rich qualitative information and the opportunity to identify problematic behavioral patterns (e.g., items involving interpersonal contact may be highly endorsed on the pleasantness dimension, but may actually be occurring on an infrequent basis).

Once patterns have been identified, target areas for treatment can more easily be specified. Also, once the client learns to translate a particular problem into one or two Tracking Sheet items, he will have taken a major step toward operationalizing the problem-solving approach.

The Tracking Sheets should be scanned in each session and inquiry made about any items consistently left blank. These may be unproductive items that should be replaced, or they may signal a new area for intervention. It is useful for the therapist to retain these Tracking Sheets and examine total and individual item changes across time. This is helpful for developing future goals and other treatment plans.

An additional use of the Tracking Sheets that capitalizes on their content is based on an overall assessment conducted after at least three weeks of tracking. Point biserial correlations can be computed to determine which ten pleasant events and which ten unpleasant events correlate most highly with mood (Siegel, 1956). Alternatively, visual inspection and discussion can serve this same purpose. The reduced lists (10 events each) are very likely to be the events most deserving focus in future sessions. Tracking should continue on these items, and new ones should be added as situations change. Clients seem to find it easier to track on these shorter lists as treatment progresses.

The therapist can use this assessment information to devise new intervention strategies and to highlight the importance and meaning of these items in controlling depression. With older clients, this process has been useful in most instances, particularly when clear patterns are discernible. Whether to employ this strategy and thus reduce the size and content of the Tracking Sheets should depend on the therapist's assessment of the clinical picture at that time.

Usefulness of Tracking Sheets to the Client. The Tracking Sheets provide direct benefits to the client. (1) Completing the forms provides a daily reminder of both the quantity and quality of pleasant and unpleasant events that are occurring. (2) The client will gain skill in controlling depression as he learns to evaluate the Tracking Sheets with the therapist's guidance. (3) Tracking can be carried on independently by the client, and thus progress can continue if sessions are missed or formal therapy sessions have been concluded.

Mood Rating Form

Moods are rated on a 9-point scale; it is helpful to have the client volunteer examples of a day ranked as 1 or as 9, and to review a preceding day or two and rate them to be certain the process is understood. In addition, the client should be made aware that the Mood Rating Form should be completed at the same time each day, preferably as close to bedtime as possible and at the same time as he prepares the Tracking Sheets. The client who feels that moods vary greatly within a day should record an average for the day.

The primary purpose of daily tracking of both categories of events is to relate those events to the client's moods. Typically, a positive relationship will be found between increased pleasant events and mood, and a negative relationship between frequent unpleasant events and mood. The therapist can use this empirically-derived relationship to illustrate the relationship between depression and quantity and quality of activities.

Behavioral Graphing: Pleasant and Unpleasant Activities/ Mood Ratings

The graph is an effective way to display visually the recorded relationships between pleasant and unpleasant events and mood. Thus, it provides a tangible means of underscoring the rationale of behavioral therapy, and at the same time monitoring the client's progress in decreasing unpleasant events and increasing those which are pleasant. The therapist should demonstrate the graphing technique and have the client practise the task during the introductory session. The client should then prepare weekly graphs to bring to subsequent sessions. Older clients may have difficulty graphing, and several periods of trial and error may be required before they master this activity.

Relaxation Log Form

The Relaxation Log Form employs a 10-point scale. The client should be asked to give examples of events which qualify as low and high on the scale of relaxation to help in discriminating anchor points for future ratings. He is then asked to rate his degree of relaxation immediately on completing each relaxation session. Date and time of session should be recorded, and under "Comments," whether the session was a regular or covert practice session as well as whether interfering thoughts or distractions were present. These logs are then used by both client and therapist to monitor skill acquisition and identify problematic situations requiring other kinds of intervention.

MEASURING TREATMENT IMPACT

Progress Notes

The therapist's progress notes are a means of keeping track of issues covered in sessions. They are used to plan future sessions and develop a continuing treatment appropriate for the individual client. Homework assigned, problems with completion of homework, and issues the client brings to the sessions should be included. Progress notes will be particularly valuable during the middle and late stages of therapy to provide the basis for selecting specific skill training areas and developing a maintenance plan.

Repeated Assessment of Depression

Administration of a self-report depression scale such as the Beck Depression Inventory (BDI) at frequent intervals is another helpful way to evaluate improvement. Clients, asked to fill out the scale without reference to prior scores, are encouraged to be as honest as possible each time. The total score can quickly be computed to index change in the overall symptom picture; this is usually encouraging to both client and therapist. In addition, scores on individual BDI items can be examined to see how they fluctuate. High scores of 2 or 3 on items should alert the clinician to specific problem areas that warrant attention.

For example, if an individual scores 3 on insomnia at the start of treatment and subsequently scores 0 or 1, this would indicate that this aspect of the depression is improving; if on the other hand the fatigability item initially is 1 and subsequently becomes a 2 or 3, the therapist should investigate what has happened in the preceding week that might account for the change. This kind of item-by-item use of the BDI seems to increase its sensitivity and assist the clinician to pinpoint areas that need immediate attention.

SUMMARY

It is important to make the proper diagnosis of the client before initiating therapy. A structured interview like the SADS is preferred, but alternative approaches have used self-report measures plus a brief clinical interview. A first step in the process is to rule out dementia and screen any individuals with psychoses or high suicidal risks. Treatment programs will be related to the diagnostic picture, and assessment of the client should be made periodically throughout treatment.

Since the Tracking Sheets, Mood Ratings, and graphs yield quantified information at every session, they should be evaluated throughout treatment to gauge the client's progress. Clearly, the effectiveness of various interventions can be determined by examining the improvements or setbacks recorded on these measures. They should be used flexibly and creatively in the service of the client. The most successful behavioral therapists have been those who integrate these data in an ongoing way, continually reevaluating where the client is coming from, where he should be going, and how to help him get there.

FOOTNOTES

[1]Copies can be obtained from Jean Endicott, Ph.D., Director, Research Assessment and Training Unit, New York State Psychiatric Institute, 722 West 168th St., New York, NY 10032. Permission of the authors must be secured prior to using this copyrighted material.

[2]Training information available from source listed in Footnote 1.

[3]Copies are obtainable from Dr. Allen Raskin, Psychopharmacology Research Branch, National Institute of Mental Health, Parklawn Bldg., Rm. 9-101, 5600 Fishers Lane, Rockville, MD 20852.

[4]Available from Dr. Gallagher.

How to Begin
Behavioral Therapy 6

The therapist should read carefully this manual, the paperback book *Control Your Depression* (Lewinsohn, Munoz, Youngren, & Zeiss, 1978), and the handouts (see Appendix) before arranging any sessions. A firm understanding of the treatment method and materials is a basic requirement for success in treatment. Questions which may arise when all the materials are considered together can thus be resolved before meeting a client with his questions.

PREPARING FOR THE FIRST SESSION

Preliminary Informal Contact

Prior to the first treatment session, it is important to make contact with the client, either by phone or during a short meeting (perhaps after the intake assessment appointment), in order to (1) reduce client uncertainty and tension, (2) provide an opportunity for answering any questions, and (3) set up a clear structure for the first therapy session.

The therapy treatment and rationale should be briefly discussed, and the client asked to plan to stay for two hours for the first session. The length of the first session should be explained: it is necessary to accomplish all that should be done at that meeting in an unhurried, relaxed spirit which will permit client and therapist to get acquainted. Mention that "breaks" can be taken during the session if necessary, since sitting in one place for over an hour can fatigue anyone and older clients may be more susceptible to such fatigue.

The therapist must get a firm verbal commitment from the client at this time to attend the first session. When making the appointment, transportation problems and physical disabilities must be considered (older persons frequently do not drive, particularly at night, and must use public transportation; they may be unable to climb stairs to a second-floor office). The conversation should end with a positive note, "I am looking forward to working with you."

Plan the Environment

Surroundings in the meeting place should be free from distractions. A comfortable chair should be supplied for the client to eliminate competition for attention from physical difficulties such as arthritis. A writing surface will be needed for activities of client and therapist throughout treatment. Variability in lighting (bright light for reading and reviewing forms and homework; reduced light for relaxation and covert rehearsal) is desirable. Many older adults need light of higher intensity to see printed or written material adequately.

If the client needs glasses for reading, he should be reminded to bring the glasses and be sure to use them. During the initial meeting or phone conversation, the clinician should attempt to ascertain whether hearing is restricted, and plan for compensation if necessary.

Review Material for Session 1

The therapist should review materials needed for Session 1 and gather them. Having everything needed at hand insures that the introductory process will run smoothly: BDI (if appropriate), "Control Your Depression" handout, client notebook and pencil, Pleasant Events Schedule, Unpleasant Events Schedule, and Daily Mood Rating Form (see Appendix).

CONDUCTING THE FIRST SESSION

If the BDI is to be used at the beginning of each session, formalize a regular procedure for its administration. Request the client to come early enough each time to pick up a blank form from the secretary. The BDI will be scored with the client and each marked item discussed to insure an understanding of client response. The BDI scores after the initial one usually drop, and this can be explained as a positive consequence of the client's engagement in treatment—a step in the right direction.

Get acquainted with the client and build the rapport necessary for treatment by reviewing the client's chief complaint and presenting problem (a brief recapitulation of the client's history based on the intake material can facilitate this process).

When a comfortable rapport has been established, clearly and precisely explain the treatment rationale (use both "Control Your Depression" handout and the outline which follows under *Treatment Rationale*). If the client knows what is coming, it will be easier for him to cooperate. Give the client a copy of the handout and let him peruse it while going through the explanation. The points listed below need not be pursued in the order listed, but be sure all information is covered.

Treatment Rationale

Behavioral treatment of depression is a psychoeducational experience which emphasizes learning certain skills. These skills, acquired one step at a time, require practice, and are intended to be used in a self-directed manner after therapy ends. Some steps or issues may seem irrelevant to the client, but the therapist should assure the client that continued practice and personalizing of techniques and homework will effect progress.

Points to be Remembered

1. **Be sure client can identify and discriminate between pleasant and unpleasant events.** Because clients may be unaccustomed to viewing experiences in this way, personal examples of these kinds of events should be solicited to insure clear understanding before administering Pleasant Events Schedule (PES) and Unpleasant Events Schedule (UES); an example follows:

> Client: "I enjoy calling my sister, but when she talks about her husband's illness, I don't enjoy it any more."
>
> Therapist: *"The phone call itself is a pleasant event, but the conversation is not pleasant, so these are really two separate events—the call is a PES item, the conversation an UES item."*
>
> Client: I don't perceive a difference, but I hadn't actually thought of that before."

> *Therapist:* "*Well, you can see its very important to distinguish what is pleasant for you and what is unpleasant for you. Knowing this, we can increase the frequency of the pleasant event only and think of ways to minimize the unpleasant nature of the conversation.*"

Explain thoroughly the relationship between pleasant events, unpleasant events, and mood. Refer to "Control Your Depression" handout for details.

2. **Express emphatically the importance of the homework.** In order for the treatment to work, homework completion is mandatory. Often older clients express dissatisfaction with their nightly assignments ("It's just too much trouble"), and they think that sufficiently justifies the omission. Strong emphasis is needed to reinforce acceptance of the fact that with daily involvement progress will be much more rapid than with only effort that takes place in the weekly sessions.

3. **Stress that use of client notebook to organize all the material client will employ in therapy is essential.** The client should be encouraged to make notes on each session and record items he wishes to discuss as they occur between sessions. The notebook will provide a place to keep all the material covered in sessions and provide a permanent record for reference in the future.

4. **Following the explanation of the rationale, have client restate the rationale in his own words** in order to insure a clear understanding of what the therapy is based on and what is likely to occur during treatment. The therapist at this time should discuss the client's expectations for treatment, comparing the behavioral method with other therapies, particularly if there has been prior psychological counseling. Older clients often expect a type of treatment where most of each session is spent discussing problems and history. These factors are integral to behavioral treatment and the therapist will be spending time talking about problems, but behavioral therapy also involves *action—doing something about the problems—*on the part of the client.

5. **Reinforce understanding that behavioral therapy for depression in older adults is designed with specified time limits.** While there is flexibility in the length of each session and the number of sessions needed to accommodate individual client or therapist, the achievement of the specific goals of behavioral treatment (increase pleasant events, decrease unpleasant events, raise mood level, and learn cognitive and behavioral skills) will be the primary factor in determining time scheduling.

6. **Emphasize collaboration by therapist and client required in behavioral therapy.** Together, they define the problem areas on which to focus and work to effect change, unlike many other models of therapy which cast the therapist either in the role of an expert or supportive listener.

7. **Set an agenda in writing at the beginning of each session.** This is necessary because of the time limits and collaborative nature of the treatment. Without such an explicit agenda, both parties may not be able to cover all the topics they wish to include in the session. Typically, the therapist can begin by stating what he needs to cover, and then ask the client if he has anything else to add. The following example is taken from an exchange during a session (Session 3).

> *Therapist:* *Today we're going to review homework, learn to graph, review your readings on relaxation, and practice relaxation. Is there anything else you would like to add?*
>
> Client: I would like to discuss the upcoming election; and also my daughter's visit, which I'm getting anxious about.
>
> *Therapist:* *I think the second item is really appropriate and can be included specifically when we are practicing the relaxation exercises in this session. However, do you have a specific reason for bringing up the election?*
>
> Client: Well, no; it was just on my mind as I was driving here.
>
> *Therapist:* *It doesn't appear directly relevant to your situation, so I think that we will shelve that for today unless you have some other special reason for talking about it. Is there anything else you wanted to mention?*
>
> Client: Well, no. That's O.K. the way you've outlined it. O.K.; let's start.

8. **Obtain the client's verbal commitment to participate and continue in treatment.** This is an essential item for the first session. Without commitment, clients cannot fully participate and a great deal of time will be lost encouraging the client to work. During the first session, the client's commitment may seem partial or half-hearted; in such a case the therapist should elicit hidden agendas or unanswered questions to encourage the commitment. Commitment is usually strengthened and reaffirmed by attendance at future sessions; therefore it is helpful to specify actual appointment dates and hours as far ahead as possible and enter them in the client's

notebook. This action will help the client to see the therapy as an ongoing process that runs a typical course, and that premature termination is undesirable. The act of entering appointments in both therapist's book and client's notebook can generate enthusiasm for the project.

9. **Anticipate for the client the difficulties inherent in the treatment system.** Interruptions and setbacks may occur. The client should understand that predictable interruptions from new crises, vacations, illnesses, or learning difficulties should not significantly interfere with the progress of treatment. These events can be dealt with in a relaxed controlled manner; learning to meet them in this way can increase the efficacy of treatment.

10. **Administer Pleasant Events Schedule and Unpleasant Events Schedule; review and add any additional events not included but which are appropriate for client.** Close this task with a restatement of future uses of this information. (See guidelines for administration, Chapter 5.)

11. **Close Session 1 with assignment of homework for next Session 2 and discussion of the focus of that meeting.** Homework consists of (1) rereading "Control Your Depression" handout and noting any questions in client notebook and (2) starting to record moods on Daily Mood Rating Form for which instructions were given in Chapter 5. In outlining the plans for Session 2 in advance, several items can be described. The therapist will have prepared specific lists of pleasant and unpleasant activities for this individual client to use in daily tracking (based on the PES and UES forms completed in Session 1). In Session 2, the client will be shown how to track. He will be asked to continue the Daily Mood Rating Forms. Other assignments may need to be developed for that specific individual, particularly if a problem existing at the start of treatment is debilitating.

CLIENT MOTIVATION

Therapists usually assume that clients are motivated to change, but this not always the case. Some older clients, who are brought to therapy by relatives or significant others who feel the client needs to change, do not themselves feel need for change. In these cases, the therapist must first determine whether the client is in fact depressed. If so, therapist and client might agree to schedule four to six sessions on a trial basis, during which time the client would be sensitized to pleasant and unpleasant events and mood ratings. This experiment will usually help to clarify whether the client is coming because of family pressure only, or because of his or her own need for treatment.

The "Yes, but . . ." position characterizes other individuals. They agree that, yes, they are depressed and want help. When the rationale, and later the specific techniques for behavioral treatment of depression are presented, the client finds all sorts of reasons why it will not work in his case, or why he cannot try. If this attitude is sensed in the initial meetings, confront the issue directly: "Are you saying that it is *impossible* to change, you can *never* relax, you have *never* changed a habit in your life?" Usually the client will reframe the original statement. Suggesting that the client consider an experimental approach which may or may not work seems to dilute the intensity of the "Yes, but . . ." position.

Finally, it is often wise to point out during Session 1 that a slump may occur during part of the treatment. Frequently older clients expect immediate change, and are disappointed and ready to quit if it does not occur. Especially with individuals who have high expectations initially, it is valuable to predict both the slump and the fact that it passes quickly. The presence of a downward trend can even serve to increase the relevance of therapy, since factors which cause the slump can be identified and worked with.

SUMMARY

Session 1 includes a great deal of material to be covered. Presenting the scheduled items in a single meeting is preferable to alternative arrangements, and usually requires a full two-hour appointment. The recommended design of the first session should ensure client compliance, start the client off on the right track, and avoid the danger that he might walk away with unanswered questions that would preclude his return for future appointments.

7 How to Complete Behavioral Therapy

TERMINATION

Because behavioral therapy is always short-term treatment, clients should be educated for termination beginning with the first session and throughout treatment. The therapist can encourage the acceptance of this time limit in several different ways; for example, he can:

1. Describe hypothetical post-treatment situations, especially when discussing the importance of generalizing skills for use outside of treatment sessions.

2. Save consideration of certain activities in which the client expresses interest (attending Weight Watchers; joining a health club) until the conclusion of therapy.

3. Periodically elicit feedback about the client's perception of progress and relate this information to his feelings about the time remaining before conclusion of therapy.

If these steps are taken, the client will have been cognitively prepared for the ending of treatment, and termination will not seem abrupt.

The actual process of termination consists of three aspects: (1) reviewing all major substantive issues covered during therapy, (2) helping the client develop self-change plans for the future, and (3) discussing feelings about the treatment and the termination directly.

Review

Several specific topics should be covered during the review portion of termination.

1. **Activity-mood graphs.** It is interesting and revealing to examine the sequential set of activity/mood graphs. This exercise

permits the client to observe progress which has been made in increasing pleasant events, decreasing unpleasant events, and improving mood level. It will provide a powerful reminder of the effect of activity level upon mood. Content as well as frequency of activities should be considered. Any trends or deviations in the types of pleasant and unpleasant activities checked on the weekly records should be noted.

2. **The problem-solving approach to dealing with feelings of depression.** It is very important for the client to be able to recognize problem situations and determine which skills are appropriate for use in a given circumstance.

3. **Specific skills learned, including relaxation.** Depending on which modules have been emphasized, the review should also cover assertiveness, communication, and cognitive control skills. How and when the various skills can be used most effectively should also be discussed.

4. **Sensitivity to the warning signs of depression.** The specific cues which accompany a downward mood swing (changes in activity level, sleep patterns, appetite, or increased tension) should be listed by the client for his review. The inevitability of stressful periods and the ameliorative steps which can be taken to cope with multiple stresses should be discussed.

Explicit Preparations

In addition to the review, which should strengthen the client's learning and his ability to apply that learning to future experiences, the following explicit preparations for the post-treatment period should be made:

1. **The client should organize his notebook so it will be readily available and comprehensible for references.** For some clients, it is desirable to schedule future meetings for reviewing the notebook.

2. **The client should be encouraged to continue any self-monitoring techniques which have proved useful.** Additional forms may need to be obtained and inserted in the notebook for easy future access.

3. **The client, with therapist help, should set some specific future goals and list the steps necessary to achieve them.** This step will increase the chances that the client will continue to progress after termination. The *process* of goal-setting should also be discussed at this time, and the importance of concrete, specific goals stressed. (An appropriate goal at this time: arranging to attend structured activities which have been deliberately delayed until the conclusion of therapy.)

Evaluating the Treatment

Encouraging the client to express his thoughts and feelings about the treatment and its ending is a final important step in therapy. The client may be finding that feelings of sadness or frustration related to termination are distorting his beliefs about the efficacy of treatment, and these feelings should be properly evaluated. Likewise, the client may experience a tendency to attribute his success in therapy to factors outside his own efforts, and the therapist can help to discourage this kind of attribution.

Some clients may not be ready to terminate treatment altogether; behavioral therapy may not have provided satisfactory symptom relief. During termination, the therapist should consider the potential benefits which might be possible through other treatment modalities and be prepared to make an appropriate referral.

Clients may request referrals for a type of treatment unrelated to the original depression (marriage counseling, sex therapy). Despite the possible value of these extra treatments, the client should be encouraged to avoid added commitments of this sort until after the follow-up period has ended in order to permit the benefits of behavioral therapy to crystallize.

FOLLOW-UP

It is important to schedule regular follow-up appointments for a time after completion of formal therapy sessions. As stated above, the client should be encouraged to avoid becoming involved in another form of treatment until after follow-up (perhaps a period of six weeks to three months). This will allow time for practising the recently-acquired skills learned in therapy and generalizing what has been learned to everyday situations. Scheduling the follow-up two or three months after termination of treatment provides an opportunity to evaluate the client's success. In addition, the client will know another appointment is scheduled, and will not need to conjure up an emergency in order to speak with the therapist.

In the follow-up interview, questions about the client's perception of current level of functioning, his current level of depression, whether any major life events or stressors have occurred in the interim, and whether the behavioral methods learned are being utilized should be raised. Clients should be reminded to bring to the follow-up appointment their notebooks and any additional tracking data and mood rating forms which will help evaluate progress over time.

The follow-up appointment will usually end by discussing whether the client feels a need to resume treatment, either behavioral therapy or another form. Results have varied among clients who participated in the U.S.C. program. (1) A number of clients did not feel the need for additional treatment. They reported that they had been able to maintain themselves quite well during the follow-up period, and in fact expressed surprise at how well they had done without the therapist's facilitation. (2) Some individuals requested additional treatment such as additional regularly scheduled "booster sessions" which they felt important to motivation and continued use of techniques. (3) Other clients expressed some irritation that the time in behavioral therapy had not permitted them to discuss all the things they wished to include, and asked for a referral to a more nondirective or supportive therapist.

MAINTAINING IMPROVEMENT

At follow-up, the clients who show that they have maintained low depression scores are those who have been able to use the techniques learned and continue their self-change efforts beyond the formal therapy sessions. They have been able to see the relevance of the behavioral approach to their daily lives, and report satisfaction with the treatment.

Individuals who report increases in depressive symptoms at follow-up have usually allowed the learned skills and self-change plans to fall into disuse. Therefore, it may be worthwhile to offer an abbreviated five or six session course of behavioral treatment which focuses on the difficulties these clients have experienced in implementing strategies and plans. For clients who cannot afford the expense of additional individual treatment, referral to a behaviorally-oriented group may be advisable.

At U.S.C., small groups are being brought together in a class called "Coping with Depression" which follows the schema of Lewinsohn et al. (1978) outlined earlier. In the small group, individuals learn the behavioral approach in a structured classroom format and reinforce each other.[1] These meetings have helped behavioral therapy "graduates" who have experienced significant negative life events (death of a spouse, for example) after individual treatment ended by providing group support and an opportunity to "brush up" on previously learned skills.

---

[1] A detailed outline of the course is available on request from Peter Lewinsohn, Ph.D., University of Oregon, Straub Hall, Eugene, Oregon. A modified version designed for use with older adults has been prepared by Larry W. Thompson, Ph.D., Andrus Gerontology Center, U.S.C., Los Angeles, and can be secured by written request.

III.

CASE

ILLUSTRATIONS

Brief comments about patients have appeared in the earlier pages of this manual to illustrate the mechanics of behavioral therapy. The case material presented for these purposes has been too specific to give a clear picture of any given client's problems or of our overall approach in applying behavioral techniques. Several cases will be presented in greater detail in this section in order to show the diversity of clients seen in our setting; these particular cases were selected specifically to indicate a number of problems which occur repeatedly in treating older persons through behavioral techniques.

Some of these clients were treated successfully; others were completely unresponsive to the behavioral approach. Although the critical ingredients which determined success or failure were not always easy to identify, in most instances the contributing factors were obvious.

Case Number 1 presents a client who had a successful therapy response typical for a substantial number of clients seen in our Center. This lady actually was responding to the therapy within three sessions, and was within the normal range on the BDI within six sessions.

Often clients either show immediate response to therapy or no response at all. In the case of clients who have not begun to respond within three or four sessions, one behavioral therapist in our acquaintance typically refers them for other kinds of therapy at that point in time. Our experience with older clients suggests that the therapist should be willing to extend the trial period beyond several sessions. However, it is helpful to keep in mind that if no change is evidenced in the first few sessions, it usually takes many sessions before significant improvement is noted.

CASE NUMBER 1

Mrs. T, an attractive 66-year-old divorcee currently in a very unsatisfactory relationship with a younger man, complained that everything was hopeless and there was "no need to go on." Over the past fifteen years this feeling had intensified periodically, yet the episodes over the past five years had been worse—so much so that there had been a suicide attempt three years ago.

Mrs. T had three grown children; two were complete disappointments to her, and she felt the third had not lived up to his potential. She felt totally responsible for her children's failures and often developed intense guilt about this.

In addition to her feelings of hopelessness, Mrs. T. also experienced a pervasive attitude that she was powerless to do anything to change her situation. She had ruined her children; now it was too late. Her husband had accused her of being a bad wife and mother; nothing she did seemed to change this. Her current relationship was going sour for similar vague reasons; she just didn't know what to do. Friends were being more distant. A recent change in job description was perceived by Mrs. T as a demotion. She sensed that the intensity of her recent distress would eventually lead to another suicide attempt, for which this time she had a more effective plan, and this was so frightening that she knew she had to get help.

Although extremely skeptical of the rationale for behavioral therapy, Mrs. T was desperate, and thus willing to try anything. During the first week of treatment and tracking of moods, the mood fluctuations she was able to discern were very surprising to her, and had an amazing impact on her attitude toward therapy. She had heretofore perceived herself as being very depressed, with no changes. Beginning therapy, she immediately caught on to the concept that if mood fluctuated, something was doing this, and that she might be able to influence an improved mood. By the end of the second week, sensitive to the events and mood connection, she had completely reversed her attitude toward the rationale. For the first time in fifteen years she felt some control over events, and the effect was extremely positive.

Mrs. T began working very hard to increase pleasant events in her life. Through the remainder of treatment, she completed all homework assignments faithfully. A major focus for change was assertion; time management skills became a relevant second area for therapeutic work.

By the end of six sessions, Mrs. T's BDI had dropped to less than 10, and it remained at that level throughout the 16-week course of therapy. She was still scoring in the non-depressed range on the BDI and other measures at the one-year follow-up appointment. At that time she reported that she had been able to ward off serious episodes of depression despite the occurrence of several negative life events during that year. She had had no recurring thoughts of suicide, and stated that if they should occur, she was now better equipped to deal with them before they became intense.

Comment

This client can be considered as one who responded successfully to behavioral treatment. The turning point seems to have occurred when, having understood and accepted the relationship between events and mood, she *experienced* that relationship and made a systematic, concerted effort to control the frequency and type of events in her life. Proceeding further to acquire additional skills in assertiveness and time management, she became able to control her moods. Continued use of these skills in her daily life after therapy had been completed prevented recurrence of depression for a whole year, with promise for extending that time indefinitely. It should be noted that this lady initially had very little enthusiasm for the rationale, but this attitude changed quickly as a result of her experience. This suggests that opinions clients hold at the outset should not be weighted too heavily in deciding whether they will respond effectively to the procedures.

CASE NUMBER 2

Mrs. B was a 57-year-old married woman with no children who worked regularly in her husband's unsuccessful retail store. Although socially isolated, she had no history of psychiatric treatment. She sought treatment because of lack of energy, problems surrounding the settlement of her deceased brother's estate, and marital discord. Mrs. B was poorly groomed; she reported symptoms such as poor appetite, constipation, insomnia, and lack of libido. She talked incessantly, digressing to explain minute details and often never returning to the central point of her narrative.

From the very beginning of treatment, Mrs. B appeared to be a poor candidate for behavioral therapy. Simply communicating the nature and course of the treatment to her proved to be an insurmountable task, because when feedback was elicited, she digressed by describing some unrelated event (usually concerning her husband's numerous faults, or the reasons she felt entitled to 100 percent of her late brother's estate).

Another early obstacle to behavioral treatment was the lack of potentially enjoyable events in her daily environment. While she could imagine being happy if major conditions in her life changed ("If my husband's business would just make money"), there were very few discrete events which she could identify as pleasant. This was further complicated by her total lack of friends.

A final clue that suggested Mrs. B might not benefit from behavioral therapy was her difficulty in grasping and accepting the notion of limited success or improvement without total recovery. Her expectations were unrealistic; for example, the only way in which she could imagine her marriage to be more satisfying was "...if things were like they were the first year we were married." Throughout treatment she was able to identify only two favors which she would appreciate from her husband: to vacuum the house, and to sort the files at work. Even here she qualified her responses: "Little things like this won't really make any difference in how I feel."

Treatment proceeded in a rather erratic fashion because (1) Mrs. B frequently cancelled or rescheduled sessions, and (2) she seldom completed (or even attempted) her homework assignments. Missed appointments curtailed any momentum achieved during preceding sessions. Failure to do homework made it impossible to progress with treatment and added to her perceptions of failure.

There was one exceptional session, distinguished by two features: it was the only week in which she had completed tracking every day, and her appearance had improved dramatically (she had gotten a haircut, and for the first time wore makeup to the session and was tastefully dressed). However, the Pleasant and Unpleasant Events Tracking Sheets, Daily Mood Ratings, and BDI score on the day of the session did not show any change from previous weeks.

Mrs. B discontinued treatment after seven sessions; she simply stopped coming in. Those seven sessions had stretched over a period of eleven weeks and had included material ordinarily covered in five weeks. Following the seventh session, she continued to call to reschedule, cancel, and reschedule again. This pattern covered several weeks. Finally, citing transportation problems, she decided "to stop coming for a while."

Mrs. B's depression score on the BDI, initially high, decreased only slightly over the course of the seven sessions, and was still quite high at the one-year follow-up.

Comment

In retrospect, several reasons for lack of success in addition to the early signs listed above can be seen.

1. Mrs. B received no cooperation or encouragement from her husband. While he was not opposed to psychotherapy, he was unwilling to drive her to sessions or rearrange her work schedule at his place of business to enable her to drive to appointments during periods of less heavy traffic on the Los Angeles freeways.

2. Another barrier to success was her need to use therapy sessions for chatting, because of her social isolation and lack of any friends.

3. It was difficult to pace the treatment to accommodate Mrs. B's slow rate of learning and to achieve the success experiences which are part of this treatment. Consequently the therapist also experienced frustration with so few successes.

Whether the behavioral modality can succeed when extended over a protracted period has not yet been empirically established. However, it is clear that brief programmed behavioral treatment was not appropriate for this client, as illustrated by the lack of change in her BDI scores over time. As shown in Figure 1, Mrs. B's score remained at the severe level throughout.

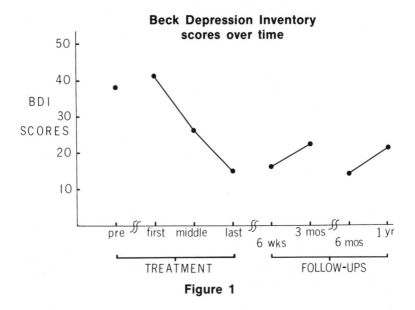

Figure 1

A final comment should be made about this client's failure to complete homework. As other behavioral therapists have frequently reported, our experience with the elderly also indicates that invariably those clients who do not do the homework do not build in the requisite skills to control depression, therefore do not show immediate or sustained benefits from therapy. This issue is so crucial that therapists should be prepared to renegotiate the size of the homework load or use any other device that will insure that the client engages in relevant behavioral activities.

Sometimes it is necessary to extend sessions and role play through the homework assignment, then call between sessions to remind clients. In one instance, the therapist called the client every night for a week to review mood monitoring for each day. The impact of this effort was sufficient to get the client started so that he could at least have the experience of monitoring long enough to see the episodic nature of his mood changes. This usually is the first step in beginning a change program.

Therapists are often inclined to overlook the older client's failure to complete homework. They do not want to push the client too much, or feel the client is not capable and do not want to embarrass him. In addition, they may feel uncomfortable admonishing their elders. Whatever the reason, if the result is incompletely reviewed or skipped homework, both therapist and client are being shortchanged.

CASE NUMBER 3

Mr. A, a 72-year-old widower who was living alone, expressed two major complaints: inactivity, and difficulty with friends. More specifically, he was concerned about his lack of motivation to clean his house and "settle in," although he had moved there five years earlier. He spent the majority of his time in bed. He had lost the friends from his previous location, and felt "used" by his lone current friend. Another aspect of his depression emerged during the second session: he was spending a great deal of time blaming himself for his problems—not having more money, not having developed a career, etc.

Through discussion, two principal goals were set: (1) to increase activity level, and (2) to increase assertive behavior in order to obtain more pleasure from his only friend and to make new friends. About halfway through the sessions it became clear that lack of self-esteem was blocking Mr. A from taking credit for progress and also limiting the pleasure he gained from increased activities. Thus, improving self-esteem became a third goal of therapy.

The first six sessions focused primarily on relaxation training. Because the client had problems with the exercises due to arthritis, the program was modified to include relaxation sessions while in the bathtub—much more successful and pleasant for him. He was also encouraged to concentrate on monitoring the situations in his life that created tension. Most of these tension-producing situations involved his relationship with his friend. Assertion training was recommended.

After the seventh appointment, sessions were changed from twice a week to once a week. About two weeks following this new schedule it became apparent that Mr. A was doing well in terms of activities and mood ratings for the first four days after a session, but then he began to slip. By the time of the next session, his level of activities and mood were again low. Discovering this, a "fantasy session" was assigned for the fourth day after the regular session. During this fantasy session he was to review his homework and the rationale of the therapy. The exercise proved very effective.

Two important techniques, time management and positive self-statements, were added during the last four weeks of therapy. Time management allowed him to break down housecleaning into manageable concrete tasks that were to be performed on specific days and at specific times. The second component took the form of positive self statements to be repeated each time he turned a page of the newspaper (which he read regularly). This assignment worked to give himself more credit for the progress he was making.

By the time therapy sessions ended, tremendous improvement could be seen through Mr. A's self-report and through the improved BDI scores (41 initially; 15 at termination). By the end of treatment he had mastered relaxation exercises, reestablished a few previous friendships, and was more assertive with his friends. He had also joined a politically active group and traveled to San Francisco and Sacramento with them. His increased energy allowed him to work more regularly on odd jobs, and this activity provided additional income which permitted him to afford more pleasant activities.

Therefore, time management and positive self-statements were to be the focus of self treatment to continue after the formal sessions ended. Scheduling of time had helped Mr. A to avoid his tendency to be overwhelmed by a task, which had been a problem earlier when faced by a large task. Positive self-statements allowed him to end self-blame and give himself credit for progress. The BDI scores for Mr. A (Figure 2) and his graph of pleasant and unpleasant activities plotted against mood ratings (Figure 3) show evidence of his improvement.

Comment

While this client still scored in the depressed range on the BDI at termination time, he showed significant improvement, having moved during the course of treatment from near incapacitation to an adequate level of functioning. Because of his longstanding and habitual inclination to evaluate himself and all his experiences negatively we were initially pessimistic about his potential for response to behavioral therapy. It was clear that he saw the rationale of the therapy, yet we thought this would be offset by the incessant negative self-statements.

Mr. A's response, much to our surprise, was extremely positive and probably as extensive as one could hope for, given his

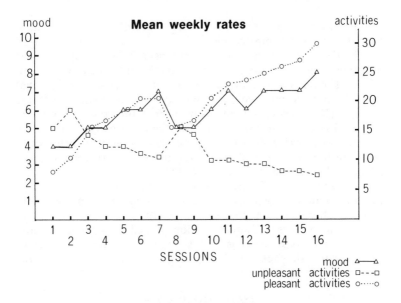

Figure 2

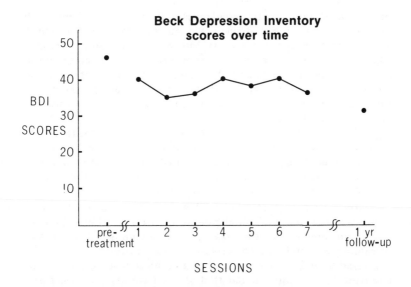

Figure 3

characteristically negative self-picture. Several factors may have contributed to his improvement.

1. He accepted the rationale for behavioral therapy. In our judgment, this has a powerful impact on the outcome of treatment.

2. The relaxation exercises in warm water provided substantial relief from a chronic problem, and gave further credibility to the therapy. (Note: Older individuals who spend time relaxing in warm water tubs should be careful to leave the tub slowly with as little exertion as possible. It is also a good idea to instruct them not to stand up too fast, particularly if they are inclined to become light-headed when doing this under normal conditions.)

3. Negative self-statements were blocking movement in therapy, and taking time to work on this early in treatment increased benefits from the other techniques.

4. The midweek fantasy session helped to refresh material covered in therapy sessions and probably minimized the client's tendency to fall back into old patterns of reacting to the many stresses he was experiencing.

CASE NUMBER 4

It is frequently assumed among mental health professionals that supportive treatment is the therapy of choice for older depressed individuals (Gerner, 1979). While our success with behavioral methods clearly challenges this assumption, there is still an unknown percentage of clients who may be unable to respond to structured therapeutic efforts but who may benefit from a traditional supportive approach. Typically, their problems seem so overwhelming to them, and their ability to change or adapt so tenuous to therapists, that they stand out as compelling examples of how some older persons are unable to cope with internal psychological stresses.

Mrs. D, a 65-year-old divorcee, came to the Center with intense psychological distress and complaints of sleep disturbance and inability to get things done. She attributed much of her trouble to a painful ulcerative condition on her feet and legs, and to the 87-year-old invalid mother who dominated her life.

Mrs. D stated that she could no longer stand her mother's oppressive control, but could not seem to do anything about it. Every morning the mother would start pounding the floor and screaming demands which Mrs. D would hasten to fulfill. She expressed hatred for her mother and a desire to just walk out of the situation, yet acknowledged that she felt totally powerless and usually wound up doing exactly as the mother demanded. Occasionally, Mrs. D became obsessed with thoughts of getting rid of her mother, but she realized this would cause incredible guilt. Such thoughts increased her feelings of worthlessness.

Mrs. D has had problems with occasional sadness, low energy level, and her mother's incessant bossiness since adolescence; never a happy person, her distress did not impair her functioning until approximately ten years earlier. At that time her son died and her husband left her; she became very lonely and depressed, and after some remission moved into a duplex with her mother. Periodic episodes of depression experienced since that time have intensified as Mrs. D's relationship with her mother and her own physical condition have deteriorated over the years.

Primary goals in Mrs. D's therapy were to become free of the mother's domination and to become more assertive in obtaining adequate medical attention for her physical problem (earlier attempts had been unsuccessful, and she felt her previous physicians had "written her off").

From the beginning, Mrs. D was skeptical about therapy, but she agreed to try the behavioral approach, However, she failed to complete any homework, and wanted to spend all the therapy time complaining about her mother and her insensitive doctors. She refused to cooperate with attempts to work out plans to change her responses to her mother, saying that no matter how hard she tried or what she did, she simply could not stand up to her mother.

After four sessions, the therapist abandoned efforts to monitor mood and activity level, and began to focus on assertive behavior in everyday situations relatively removed from Mrs. D's mother. The client complained that these were irrelevant to her problem.

Attempts to explain the rationale went unheeded so the therapist began to work on developing assertive responses specific to daily demands of the mother. Here, both imagery and role play were so stressful that they too were discarded. Mrs. D could not even tolerate the *thought* of not responding immediately when the mother banged on the floor for assistance.

Every creative attempt to engage Mrs. D in active problem-solving met with stern resistance, and frequently with agitation. However, permitting her to ventilate her feelings—nothing more— seemed to have a calming effect. This observation was shared with Mrs. D during the ninth session. She agreed that talking made her feel better, adding that the other things were of no help and perhaps another form of therapy would be more helpful, whereupon she was assigned to a paraprofessional peer counselor available in our setting.

Mrs. D and the peer counselor met for six sessions spaced about a month apart; Mrs. D reported that it was indeed helpful to have "someone to talk to." The peer counselor was as frustrated as the original therapist had been when trying to introduce behavioral changes. Still, as long as the relationship was kept strictly supportive, Mrs. D seemed to look forward to the sessions, and she reported some alleviation of her distress.

Mrs. D was evaluated one year after behavioral therapy had been discontinued. Although she was still found to be clinically depressed on various assessment instruments, she said she had come to terms with her mother and realized she had to accept the fact that things would not change until the mother died. Mrs. D was positive about the value of her contacts with the peer counselor, and although sessions were infrequent, she intended to maintain that relationship.

Comment

While Mrs. D emphatically declared that she wanted things to be different in her life, she was clearly negativistic and resisted structured suggestions made by the therapist. Gallagher and Frankel (1980) describe this type of elderly individual as reflecting a "metacomplementary" style of interaction; they suggest that any therapy focusing directly on change may indeed be difficult to implement with such clients. If this pattern of "yes-but" responses becomes evident in the early stages of therapy, it may be helpful to present more limited goals and to proceed with a less structured and more supportive program. A real danger here is that the therapist may prejudge the client as unwilling and/or unable to work toward change simply because of a client's initial negative attitude. Many elderly individuals are skeptical about "talking therapies," and they will continue to verbalize this skepticism even though they are participating wholeheartedly with the therapist in a collaborative therapeutic process. It is not uncommon to have an older client perform all homework, collaborate with the therapist in many or all of the difficult exercises, show noticeable changes in daily living patterns and depressive symptomatology, and yet remain convinced that nothing is happening in therapy. This seems to be due to a "lag factor" similar to that reported by Berger and Rose (1977), which means that attributions about change tend to lag behind actual behavior changes. Perception of change may require environmental feedback, which often is not immediate, before it becomes a more integral part of the person. In such instances it is important for the therapist to remain objective and focus on positive changes which have occurred; pointing out the lag factor can be helpful with some clients as well.

CASE NUMBER 5

Case Number 5 illustrates some of the difficulties older persons have at night. The most common complaint among older depressed persons, particularly widows and widowers, is loneliness. This problem is heightened during the night when they cannot sleep and there is no one to talk with or just be with. The resulting psychological distress at times becomes acutely intense and may precipitate a variety of psychological or (as in this case) psychosomatic reactions.

Mrs. P, an active 70-year-old widow, began treatment because of a long history of "panic attacks." These attacks, which usually came on suddenly in the middle of the night and lasted for several hours at a time, sometimes occurred as often as three times in a single night. During the attacks she suffered palpitations, shortness of breath, profuse sweating, coldness and pallor of face and extremities, and a strong feeling of imminent death.

Although Mrs. P knew that these attacks always subsided in time, an overwhelming fear of dying prompted her at times to telephone various emergency helplines in an effort to speak with a professional person until the attack subsided. On at least two occasions she became so upset and anxious that she called paramedics for assistance; after being rushed to a hospital and thoroughly evaluated, physicians could find no physiological cause for her symptoms.

Mrs. P eventually accepted the fact that her panic attacks were primarily psychological in nature, but felt she could never gain control over them or live a normal life again. She was depressed at her inability to help herself, and feelings of helplessness and hopelessness about her future intensified. She decided to seek psychological help at a point when the attacks were frequent and she recognized that she was feeling very bad about herself.

The goals of Mrs. P's treatment, set early, changed relatively little throughout therapy. The first goal was to reduce the intensity and duration of the panic attacks by using relaxation techniques; she was to learn basic relaxation skills in the office and apply them whenever she found herself having an attack or believed one might be imminent. The second goal of therapy was to improve her relationships with her married adult children. Interestingly, she never called them when experiencing an attack despite the fact that they lived in the immediate area. With the therapist, she expressed her feelings that they had no respect for her and would not support a plan she had been developing to move to another state to live with a sibling with whom she felt a closeness. Apparently she had been unable to express her feelings to her children honestly, and thus the second focus of treatment concerned her lack of assertiveness with her family. Possessing effective assertion and communication skills which she applied comfortably in everyday situations, she needed to learn to utilize these skills appropriately in the domestic arena.

Mrs. P was able to learn the relaxation techniques aimed at managing the panic attacks very quickly in the initial sessions of behavioral therapy, and her BDI scores dropped from an initial 25 to about 18. However, she found it difficult to apply these techniques to the nocturnal attacks. She continued to make nightly calls to an emergency phone service connected with the Adult Counseling Center at the Andrus Center without even trying the relaxation techniques on her own, and this practice presented a new problem. Not only was she failing to control her panic attacks, but she was also talking with other therapists who rotated in the on-call function and who were unaware of her treatment plan. They were unprepared to deal with her particular problem as well as the duration of her calls.

To remedy this situation, specific directions outlining how Mrs. P's emergency calls were to be handled were drafted and distributed to the on-call personnel and the client herself. When Mrs. P called, she was to be encouraged and assisted in beginning her relaxation procedures; she' and the emergency staff person were to spend no more than ten minutes on the telephone. Initially, Mrs. P protested strenuously about the time limit; talking for an hour or more had helped her to calm down and make it through the rest of the night. However, after several calls and further protests, she accepted these behavioral limits and eventually expressed gratitude for the plan and the encouragement it gave her to assume responsibility for the panic attacks and learn that she herself could control them.

By the eighth session of treatment, Mrs. P's attacks had dropped in intensity, duration, and frequency, occurring on an average of only once per week. She was effectively handling them with minimal outside assistance. When her BDI, which dropped steadily during this period, reached the "mildly depressed" range, the therapist decided to move to the second goal.

The next six sessions focused on constructing and implementing a hierarchy of assertive responses to use with Mrs. P's adult chilren. Role playing, the most frequent technique used, was followed by role reversal in the later sessions. Mrs. P began with the least threatening statements she wanted to make to her daughters and ended with the most threatening item, her planned out-of-state move. Each set of responses was well rehearsed with the therapist before confronting the family. Mrs. P was then able to communicate more effectively with her family, who in turn responded quite favorably to her efforts to be honest with them. By the end of treatment, her BDI scores were well into the non-depressed range, averaging between 2 and 5 at termination.

Comments

Mrs. P's case was considered a very successful example of the benefits possible with behavioral therapy. Learning behavioral techniques permitted Mrs. P, not only to reduce her panic attacks, but to eliminate them entirely before treatment sessions ended. She credited the protocol distributed to the nighttime on-call personnel as being a key ingredient in effecting her control of the nightly anxiety. She reported that once she knew she wasn't going to get a sympathetic ear, there was no reason to waste time; that she might as well begin relaxation procedures comfortably, alone, and in control.

Mrs. P's assertiveness with her family clearly improved their overall relationship, and led them to support and approve her contemplated move. At three-month and six-month follow-ups conducted by phone following the move, Mrs. P was continuing to do well, with no significant depression or anxiety reported.

CASE NUMBER 6

Finally, Case Number 6 illustrates a difficulty frequently encountered: enmeshed family systems which are counterproductive to therapeutic aims. While often families can be enlisted to assist in the therapeutic process, at times this is not the case.

Mr. J, a retired 69-year-old pharmacist, complained of serious depression and inability to think straight or get anything done. His wife, completely exasperated with him, stated that all he did was "lie around like a vegetable." He would not talk with her, help with anything in the house; he did not seem to appreciate attempts to cheer him up. It was almost impossible to get him out of bed, and when he did get up and try to do something, he seemed to become confused. Mrs. J was fearful that he might be becoming senile.

Mr. J's initial BDI score, 39, was in the severely depressed range. His performance on a standard mental status examination indicated some problem with delayed memory, but he was well oriented. Advised to have a thorough physical evaluation to rule out possible organic problems, the appropriate studies turned out to be negative. It thus appeared that his problems in processing information were probably due to depression rather than organic.

Because there was some concern that behavioral therapy might not have an immediate impact due to Mr. J's low activity level, he and his wife were alerted not to expect quick results. Nevertheless, Mr. J seemed mildly enthusiastic and agreed to try behavioral therapy.

The first goal was to encourage more activity, especially of kinds that would lead to pleasant occurrences. During the first week of treatment it became apparent that none of the things he was doing around the house gave him enjoyment. Part of the problem seemed to be that he was always in his wife's way; she complained she could not get things done; she had to attend to him and clean up after him, and frequently commented that she wished he were back at work so she could have some peace and quiet. Efforts were made to obtain her cooperation in structuring positive activities for Mr. J during subsequent weeks. After the first few attempts she refused, saying she just did not have the time, and that he was the one who should be doing something, not she.

By the end of the third week, Mr. J was having difficulty completing any homework assignments designed to increase activity. While he seemed to be less distressed and confused, his wife was more obviously angry with him, and this was beginning to worry him. Mrs. J was again approached by the therapist, this time to discuss the importance of trying to control her anger. She agreed to cooperate; she seemed genuinely sorry about her agitation toward her husband, but added that having him around in his condition was terribly upsetting and frustrating.

Several days later, Mrs. J called to cancel Mr. J's next appointment, feeling that behavioral therapy was not helping him and that he needed medication. She stated that she had made an appointment with a psychiatrist, and would be taking Mr. J there on the day of his cancelled appointment.

Mr. J's BDI on the last visit was 34, still in the severely depressed range. Several calls following up after his termination have indicated that medication seemed to help and that he no longer was interested in behavioral therapy. At the one-year follow-up, Mr. J was still on medication, and also was attending a psychiatric day care program four days each week. His BDI, 30, was still high, but he said he felt better and had a little more energy. Also, he commented that he thought it was easier on his wife to be in the day care center for those days each week.

Comments

We view this case as unsuccessful, because Mr. J dropped out of treatment with significant depression still apparent. Several factors appear to be responsible for the negative outcome: his wife's lack of cooperation and inability to become involved in the treatment program coupled with Mr. J's extremely low energy level and his anxiety about doing things around the home that might anger his wife. A combination of these elements apparently led to their decision to terminate behavioral treatment prematurely.

Mr. J appears to be somewhat improved on the current treatment plan of medication plus participation in a psychiatric day treatment center, yet even with this intensive regime, his depression is still clinically significant. One might argue that behavioral treatment did not stand a chance in this case, given the complex dynamics of the marital situation, and that possibly a systems approach to treatment which involved Mrs. J as well as her husband would have been more appropriate. Since this approach was not attempted, it is impossible to judge whether it would have been more effective in this instance.

IV.

SESSION BY SESSION

WORKBOOK

This workbook presents, in outline form, procedures and materials needed to conduct behavioral therapy with older clients through sixteen sessions. The number of sessions has been set at sixteen because that number of meetings usually provides adequate time to present many significant behavioral skills. Sixteen is not to be considered a "magic" number, however; clients differ a great deal in their degree of distress and commitment to therapy, and therapists differ in their ability to establish rapport and communicate. Because of these factors, the content specified for a given session may require amplification, and two or three hours may be necessary for the material to be covered in depth. Thus, the actual number of sessions required will vary from person to person.

Another critical factor in determining the pace of therapy is clients' varying needs to talk about recent significant events in their lives and their resulting feelings. It is essential to obtain feedback at each session and to structure the meeting to insure that clients have enough time to talk through problems. If this element is missing, older clients may become disenchanted and terminate therapy before they come to appreciate its value. The amount of time per session needed for such discussion and feedback may recommend extending the total number of sessions. Remember, it is important that the various steps outlined for each session are accomplished before moving on to new material.

During the first six sessions, therapy concentrates on the basic components which will provide the foundation for subsequent problem-solving phases of the program: (1) specific techniques for monitoring mood and activities, and for pinpointing problem areas are taught, and (2) standard relaxation procedures, including both overt and covert techniques, are introduced and practiced. Methods are comparable for all clients, although specific content will obviously vary, as will the amount of "talk time" needed by the client in each of these preliminary sessions.

Emphasis in the next six sessions is on identifying specific problems and then acquiring and applying the appropriate behavioral skills needed for resolving them. Sessions become more individualized as the strengths and weaknesses of the client's current behavioral skill repertoire are assessed and one or more of the various skill training approaches are introduced. Typically, as progress occurs, the need for "talk time" is reduced and considerable skill training can be accomplished.

The final four sessions focus on problems and issues which are relatively common and require attention in all clients (such as how to continue progress after formal treatment ends). Progress tends to be significant at this point in treatment as the client assumes greater responsibility for both his behavior and his moods.

SESSION 1

(Requires 1½ - 2 hours)

1. Administer Beck Depression Inventory (BDI), and compare with intake BDI score.
2. Review chief complaint or presenting problem; get acquainted with client.
3. Explain treatment rationale (use "Control Your Depression" handout).
   A. Deal with client's expectations re treatment; compare with other treatments to which he/she may have been exposed.
   B. Explain time-limited nature of treatment (total length of time; number of sessions). Stress need to stay with agenda, which may require periodic interruptions. Set up timetable of sessions and record it in client's notebook.
   C. Discuss learning model and emphasis on skill acquisition and building.
   D. Explain necessity for regular completion of homework assignments in order to make progress.
   E. Introduce use of notebook as form of organizing homework material and keeping permanent record of materials covered in therapy sessions.
   F. Elicit feedback, answer questions, ask for restatement of rationale in client's own words.

4. Obtain client's verbal commitment to follow program as outlined above. (THIS IS ESSENTIAL BEFORE PROCEEDING FURTHER; TAKE THE NECESSARY TIME TO ESTABLISH COMMITMENT.)
5. Give client Pleasant Events Schedule (PES) and Unpleasant Events Schedule (UES) forms to complete. Explain their future use; illustrate until client understands task. Leave room and return periodically to insure accurate completion. Review forms with client to insure that *all* items are completed. Elicit additional items relevant to this specific client which may not appear in the forms.
6. Give client first homework assignment.
   A. Daily Mood Rating Form (DMR)—explain and have client rate moods for session day and preceding day as examples.
   B. Have client read "Control Your Depression," and record in his notebook any questions he may have about it.
7. Tell client that next session will be devoted to:
   A. Discussion of PES/UES
   B. Explanation of Pleasant and Unpleasant Activities Tracking Sheets
   C. Brief introduction to relaxation
8. Close session by asking client if he has any questions or general feedback as to how the session went. Reconfirm next appointment date.

Note: In subsequent sessions, general "talk time" is subsumed under agenda-setting. See Chapter 4, section on "Constructive Use of Therapy Time," for discussion of how this is done.

THERAPIST'S HOMEWORK FOR SESSION 2

1. Record progress notes for Session 1.
2. Score PES and UES.
3. Generate preliminary Pleasant and Unpleasant Activities Tracking Sheets. Include all individualized items added by client. (Lists will be used flexibly, and items may be tailored or substituted later to meet client's specific needs or interests.)
4. Collect forms for Session 2.
   A. BDI
   B. "Learning to Get Completely Relaxed" handout
   C. Pleasant and Unpleasant Activities Tracking Sheets therapist has prepared

SESSION 2

Optional: Administer BDI (see Session 1, 1A).
1. Set agenda with client's collaboration.
2. Review homework (Daily Mood Rating Form, "Control Your Depression" handout).
3. Explain how Pleasant and Unpleasant Activities Tracking Sheets were generated.
   A. Explain how daily monitoring of activities and mood will be used to determine treatment progress (decrease in occurrence of unpleasant events, increase in occurrence of pleasant events should relate to improved mood).
   B. Demonstrate use of Tracking Sheets by having client track previous day's activities. (Allow at least half the session for this because many items will need to be personalized with specific examples relevant to this client.)
4. Compare client PES and UES scores (frequency, enjoyability/ aversiveness, and cross products) with age norms if therapist feels this would have meaning for client. (Some clients grasp this notion more easily than others; use your discretion re the usefulness of this technique.)
5. Tell client the next session will be devoted mostly to relaxation training. Explain the rationale for early focus on how to relax: tenseness can exacerbate aversiveness of unpleasant situations and hinder one from learning new skills to decrease aversiveness. The client will learn how to relax, then learn how to apply relaxation skills to real life situations. Hand out "Learning to Get Completely Relaxed."
6. Assign homework:
   A. Begin tracking on Pleasant and Unpleasant Activities Tracking Sheets.
   B. Continue Daily Mood Rating Forms.
   C. Read new handout. Emphasize that correct order should be memorized. (If client uses or has used other relaxation method such as transcendental meditation, Zen, yoga, autogenic training, progressive relaxation, hypnosis, etc., reinforce by asking how it worked.) Whatever works best for the client is the important concern; however, ask the client to try the system described in "Learning How to Get Completely Relaxed" for evaluation purposes. This progressive muscular relaxation technique was developed by Dr. Gerald R. Rosen and can be found in *The Relaxation Book: An Illustrated Self-help Program* published by Prentice Hall, Inc., Englewood Cliffs, NJ 07632.

7. Close session by asking client if he has any questions or feedback as to how therapy is proceeding. Reconfirm next appointment date.

THERAPIST'S HOMEWORK FOR SESSION 3

1. Record progress notes.
2. Have relaxation tape ready.
3. Prepare revised Pleasant and Unpleasant Activities Tracking Sheets, if necessary (i.e., if in Session 2 many items needed to be revised or to be highly personalized).
4. Collect materials:
    A. Relaxation log sheet
    B. Revised Tracking Sheets therapist has prepared
    C. Good graph paper and multicolored pens or pencils.

SESSION 3

Optional: Administer BDI.
1. Set agenda with client's collaboration.
2. Review Daily Mood Rating Form.
3. Review Pleasant and Unpleasant Activities Tracking Sheets item by item. Answer questions regarding types of events that should be marked. Modify wording of items if necessary to make the item more specific for that client. Write in new items as necessary to individualize the Tracking Sheets as much as possible. Review instructions and encourage accurate completion of form *daily* until next session.
4. Review how mood ratings were determined by client. Answer questions and clarify, so mood ratings will become an accurate reflection of the client's affective status.
5. Graph Frequency of Pleasant and Unpleasant Activities. Use colored pencils. Therapist should plot first two days, client remaining days. Spend time discussing the relationship observed, and tie this in with the general treatment rationale.
6. Review rationale of "Learning How to Get Completely Relaxed." Answer questions and clarify problems. Check whether client has learned order of muscle relaxation; review order using form, "Method for Creating Tension." With client, complete form by demonstrating methods for creating tension and relaxation for each muscle group in order. What works for this particular client should be noted on form, and form should be placed in client notebook.
7. Provide first relaxation training session. Emphasize relaxation as a general skill and acknowledge that this skill acquisition phase

may require more than one session for mastery of the technique. It is advisable to slowly go through each muscle group and solicit client feedback on the learning process before proceeding to the next group.

A. Have client get into comfortable position.
B. Lead client through relaxation procedure; stop periodically if tension or discomfort are noticed to ask for feedback. Therapist has several options for carrying out this procedure:
    1. Read procedure from handout.
    2. Play a standard relaxation tape or therapist's own tape.
    3. Use any relaxation program comfortable for therapist and effective for client.
    Therapist may wish to:
    1. Give client a suitable tape for learning relaxation techniques at home.
    2. Ask client to make his own tape to encourage self-instruction.
    3. Give client a tape to be used primarily to relax rather than as a learning method (this decision will depend on client preference and learning skills).
C. Make sure client is relaxed by end of session.
D. Make sure client understands how to accomplish relaxation by himself, either by using a tape or remembering steps.
E. Inform client next session will be devoted to a review of relaxation in which client will demonstrate chosen relaxation technique.

8. Assign homework:
A. Continue daily recording on Pleasant and Unpleasant Activities Tracking Sheets.
B. Continue Daily Mood Rating Form.
C. Graph Mood Ratings against daily frequency of Pleasant and Unpleasant Activities.
D. Read "Learning How to Get Completely Relaxed" again. Provide client with Relaxation Log Sheet (see Appendix). Direct client to schedule one, and preferably two, relaxation sessions per day. Have client record sessions on log and rate each session according to degree of relaxation (rating system described in Log Sheet), and bring the Relaxation Log Sheet to all future sessions.

9. Close session by asking for feedback from client. Reconfirm next appointment.

THERAPIST'S HOMEWORK FOR SESSION 4

1. Record progress notes.
2. Review Pleasant and Unpleasant Activities Tracking Sheets; note recurring, consistent patterns to help client in future sessions to pinpoint activities which should be decreased or increased.
3. Obtain copy of "How to Relax in Real-Life Situations."

SESSION 4

Optional: Administer BDI.
1. Set agenda with client's collaboration.
2. Review homework (Pleasant and Unpleasant Activities Tracking Sheets, Daily Mood Ratings, graph of Activity Level and Mood. Relaxation Log). Client now should be able to perform the mechanics of recording information properly, so therapist can focus on qualitative analysis of data. For example, on Pleasant and Unpleasant Activities Tracking Sheets, attention should be directed toward specific patterns of activities that show a definite relationship to mood for the client.
3. Review Relaxation Log. Was client able to complete form? If not, address any specific problems encountered. Has client progressed toward becoming more relaxed through the home relaxation sessions? Discuss results and problems; pay special attention to times when relaxation rating was especially high or low.
4. Have client demonstrate relaxation procedures, going through the entire process with therapist observing. Client should verbally self-instruct so therapist can give feedback. If client has difficulty getting past a particular muscle group, the therapist may interject suggestions for restructuring technique and make relaxation more effective. This activity will require the balance of the session.
5. Inform client that the next session will focus on an unpleasant event which produces much tension and/or anxiety, and will consist of learning how to decrease these feelings through relaxation skills.
6. Assign homework:
   A. Continue daily recording on Pleasant and Unpleasant Activities Tracking Sheets.
   B. Continue Daily Mood Rating Form.
   C. Continue Relaxation Log.

D. Ask the client to prepare covert relaxation for the next session: imagine being relaxed in a real-life situation of tension. Have client read "How to Relax in Real-life Situations" up to section on relaxing in actual situations. Prior to the next session, have client pinpoint a specific situation in which he or she wishes to be relaxed.

7. Close session by asking client whether he has any questions or feedback. Reconfirm next appointment.

THERAPIST'S HOMEWORK FOR SESSION 5

1. Record progress note.
2. Read handout, "How to Relax in Real-life Situations" prior to Session 5.
3. Obtain copy of "Creating a Personal Plan to Overcome Depression" to give to client in Session 5.
4. Underline anything in "Creating a Personal Plan..." that might be relevant for client when giving handout to client at Session 5.

SESSION 5

Optional: Administer BDI.

1. Set agenda in collaboration with client.
2. Review homework. This includes analysis of Pleasant and Unpleasant Activities Tracking Sheets, Daily Mood Ratings, graph plotting, relaxation log, handout on "How to Relax in Real-life Situations" as well as the selected actual situation on which the client chose to work. Keep in mind that relaxation level should be increasing; if for any reason it declines, therapist must address this before proceeding.
3. Elicit questions and client response to "How to Relax in Real-life Situations." Before starting, briefly review the technique involved and select the specific aversive situation on which the client wishes to work. Use handout to go through Steps 1-4.
4. When Steps 1-4 are clear, proceed to Step 5 (imagine or covertly rehearse the sequence the client specified).

The aim of this session is to have client learn the technique of covert rehearsal. Have client get in a relaxed position and verbalize his imagining of the situation as well as his behavior in the situation (the imagining should include positive outcomes). After client does this once, therapist should elicit feedback as to how comfortable client felt. Then therapist should offer any observations which might facilitate client's ability to deal with situation in the most positive manner. If time permits, have client repeat Step 5, with focus on a different aversive situation.

5. Inform client that next session will focus on (1) preparing to use relaxation skills in *actual* situations and (2) choosing a specific problem area that is a major source of the client's depression.
6. Assign homework:
   A. Have client schedule 2 sessions of covert relaxation each day.
   B. Have client log relaxation sessions of Relaxation Log.
   C. Have client read section on "Relaxing in Actual Situations" in "How to Relax" handout.
   D. Have client read "Creating a Personal Plan to Overcome Depression." This handout outlines in simple language several common problem areas associated with depression and conveys the idea that most problems can be tackled through learning specific, relevant skills. The material should be read actively with the objective of having the client select a salient area to discuss during the next session. This handout often stimulates self-reflection which can be helpful in prioritizing areas to work on and establishing reasonable goals.
7. Close session by asking for questions and feedback. Reconfirm next appointment.

THERAPIST'S HOMEWORK FOR SESSION 6

1. Record progress notes.
2. Read "Creating a Personal Plan to Overcome Depression."
3. Obtain copy of Skill Training Situation Form.

SESSION 6

1. Set agenda in collaboration with client.
2. Review homework (Pleasant and Unpleasant Activities Tracking Sheets, Daily Mood Ratings, Graph of Activities and Mood, Relaxation Log). Pay particular attention to covert rehearsal relaxation session. Answer questions and provide appropriate feedback on homework.
3. Review "How to Relax in Real-Life Situations." Work with client to have him *use* relaxation in a situation which has been practiced covertly. Discuss with client ways of using what he has covertly practiced in a real-life situation. Explore with client when this situation will occur, and schedule a time for client to implement this skill "in vivo." Have client schedule a covert relaxation practice session prior to the in vivo session. Have client begin to log covert relaxation sessions on the Covert Rehearsal Practice Record; also, have client continue to log regular relaxation sessions. Both are necessary for tracking improvement.

4. Before reviewing handout "Creating a Personal Plan to Overcome Depression" and the client's specific notations, discuss the rationale of the problem-solving approach to treatment of depression. Utilization of a problem-solving approach entails:
   A. Identify/pinpoint specific problematic situations.
   B. Look at what precipitates the situation and what reactions client has (antecedent and consequent factors).
   C. Look at possible solutions client has used or considered using.
   D. Select the most appropriate solutions.
   E. Determine skills required to implement these solutions. (For example, in order to decrease occurrence and diversity of problem interactions, client might need to strengthen communication skills, assertiveness skills, decisionmaking skills, and/or cognitive self-control skills. Any one or combination of these may be relevant for the specific individual.)
5. In this session, therapist needs to assist client in applying this model to an easily solved problem with a high probability of success. This enables client to learn the approach, so that later he can apply it to more complex real-life situations as treatment progresses.
6. Review client's notations on "Creating a Personal Plan to Overcome Depression" so that a clearly relevant problem area can be selected, one which is amenable to the problem-solving approach outlined above. *This is a critical point in treatment,* at which time the therapist can best assist the client by drawing on accumulated information about client's strength and weakness, and by using his clinical judgment to carefully pinpoint skills the client needs to strengthen. To accomplish this, therapist needs to review a number of sources of information:
   (1) Comparison of Mood Ratings in conjunction with Pleasant and Unpleasant Activities Tracking Sheets (visual examination of weekly charts).
   (2) Overt and covert Relaxation Logs.
   (3) Therapist's impression of client based on experience with individual during course of therapy.
7. This session should conclude with a decision about which skill training area(s) should receive focus in coming sessions. Inform client that subsequent sessions will emphasize the relevant specific training modules.
8. Assign homework:
   A. Continue Pleasant and Unpleasant Activities Tracking Sheets.
   B. Continue Mood Ratings.

C. Continue Relaxation Log.

D. Complete Skill Training Situation Form. This form asks client to relate a concrete situation—an example of the skill training area to receive focus in Session 7.

9. Close session by asking for questions and feedback. Reconfirm next appointment.

THERAPIST'S HOMEWORK FOR SESSIONS 7-12

1. Record progress notes.
2. Select and prepare appropriate Skills Training Area(s) to be used in subsequent sessions.

SESSIONS 7-12

See Skills Training Areas Section following Session 16.

THERAPIST'S HOMEWORK FOR SESSION 13

1. Record progress notes.
2. Obtain copies of Daily Plan Sheets.
3. Obtain copy of *How to Get Control of Your Time and Your Life* by Alan Lakein, New American Library (paperback), 1973, for reference during Session 13.
4. Obtain aids for Daily Plan Sheets (colored pens, pencils).

SESSION 13

1. Set agenda with client's collaboration.
2. Review homework.
3. Survey/review what has been done in skill training sessions. List skills learned and types of situations in which they have been most helpful.
4. Begin work on Time Management, final skill to be developed in treatment. Discuss importance of *planning* to achieve a balance between pleasant (enjoyable, important to self, valued) versus unpleasant (have to, not enjoyable) activities, as well as the importance of comfortable, flexible use of time.
5. Therapist must recognize and accommodate wide variation in client ability to make use of time management skills. Some older clients have benefited from a modified version of the Lakein system, with time management organized around short term goals and immediate planning of pleasant activities. For other clients with more resources and greater time demands, therapist may recommend a more in-depth involvement in the Lakein strategies. Whether to assign reading of entire book or relevant

sections will depend on client. Two techniques found useful for all clients have been (1) prioritizing daily events, and (2) weekly division and planning of "have to" and "want to" activities to insure scheduling of pleasant activities in each day.

6. Using Daily Plan Sheets, help client schedule activities for coming week.

    A. List routine activites (breakfast, dinner).

    B. List all "have to" activities (house cleaning, shopping)—core activities that do not change time slots from week to week.

    C. Schedule "have to" activities on Daily Plan Sheets. See that there are sufficient time slots available for pleasant "want to" activities; if not sufficient time available, prioritizing activities here is essential.

    D. List all "want to" activities (going to a movie). If there are many, therapist may have client prioritize these. Usually there are few enough so they can be included in the week.

    E. Therapist may wish to distinguish between "have to" and "want to" activities on Daily Plan Sheets by use of different color pens or other similar visual aids.

7. Assign homework:

    A. Continue recording on Pleasant and Unpleasant Activities Tracking Sheets and Daily Mood Rating Form.

    B. Encourage client to follow plan outlined on Daily Planning Sheet, and to record on separate Daily Planning Sheet actual activities done for the week.

8. Close session by asking for feedback from client. Reconfirm next appointment.

THERAPIST'S HOMEWORK FOR SESSION 14

1. Record progress notes.
2. Do any additional review of time management techniques necessary at this point.

SESSION 14

1. Set agenda in collaboration with client.
2. Review homework (Pleasant and Unpleasant Activities Tracking Sheets, Daily Mood Ratings, Daily Plan Sheets).
3. Evaluate time management plans for past week. Contrast plan designed in prior session with actual activities accomplished to check accuracy in planning and insure a balance between "want to" and "have to" activities. Discuss time management problems, and reinforce main points of the technique.
4. Using Daily Plan Sheets, have client plan coming week to better conform with what he is able to do (is client using too little or too

much time for a particular activity; is time allotted realistically, are activities balanced?).
5. Help client generalize notion of planning to areas of life other than time management (meal planning for a client concerned about weight, but without experience planning menus by the week, for example).
6. Assign homework:
   A. Continue tracking on Pleasant and Unpleasant Activity Sheets and Daily Mood Rating Form.
   B. Have client review his notebook to prepare for termination (techniques, problems, stumbling blocks).
7. Close session by asking for specific feedback. Reconfirm next appointment.

THERAPIST'S HOMEWORK FOR SESSION 15

1. Record progress notes.
2. Review case file. Note significant problem areas and techniques effective for this client to prepare for maintenance planning, the focus of Session 15.

SESSION 15

Optional: Administer BDI.
1. Set agenda in collaboration with client.
2. Review homework (Daily Plan Sheets, Pleasant and Unpleasant Activities Tracking Sheets, Daily Mood Rating Form).
3. Review progress of treatment; assess success of strategies and tactics.
   A. Decreasing unpleasant events
      1. Was client able to decrease frequency and aversiveness of unpleasant events?
      2. Did such decreases result in improved mood?
      3. Are these decreases being maintained?
      4. What tactics or skills did client find helpful?
      5. Any related problems?
   B. Increasing pleasant events
      1. Was client able to increase frequency and enjoyment of pleasant events?
      2. Did such an increase result in improved mood?
      3. Are these increases being maintained?
      4. What tactics or skills did client find helpful?
      5. Any related problems?
4. Elicit feelings about upcoming termination of formal treatment sessions. Assist client in making this transition by reviewing

learning that has occurred and by reminding client that progress has been achieved primarily through his own efforts, and therefore that progress can continue as long as client *uses* what has been learned.

5. Use remainder of session to develop a maintenance and prevention program with client. Solicit client ideas on how to structure a successful program; provide therapist feedback and ideas. The plan might include continuation on some regular basis of the monitoring of events and mood and the techniques which ave been used and found helpful, as welll as the strategies for dealing with potentially stressful, difficult situations that might arise in the future. The goal is to have the client develop a systematic treatment plan to (1) maintain gains and continue to use skills learned in treatment and (2) to be alert to and avoid recurrence of depression.

6. Close session by asking for feedback. Reconfirm next appointment.

THERAPIST'S HOMEWORK FOR SESSION 16

1. Record progress notes.
2. Review all case material to be sure that no significant problem areas have been overlooked in the maintenance plan development.

SESSION 16

1. Re-administer BDI (or similar self-rating depression measure) to compare depression level at beginning of treatment with current level; this usually shows considerable progress.
2. Set agenda in collaboration with client.
3. Review final homework.
4. Use remainder of session to solidify maintenance/prevention program. Ask client which skills have been most helpful; which he would like to continue to use, and in what ways; what plans he has for maintaining present mood level and dealing with possible future stressful situations. Spend any extra time talking about other client concerns.
5. Inform client that maintenance/prevention program will be reviewed at future follow-up sessions. Recommend that follow-up sessions be held at systematic intervals (e.g., every month, or every three months), and set up appointments at this time. Follow-up sessions need not be structured in advance. If new problems have arisen in the interim, already-learned techniques should be reviewed and client assisted in applying them.

SKILLS TRAINING AREAS
FOR
SESSIONS 7-12

At this juncture in treatment, older clients often are not convinced that learning additional behavioral skills will resolve the problems that required them to seek therapy. They still see their problems "globally"; for example, "I feel bad; I don't know what to do with my time. There's nothing to enjoy any more." Therefore, if skills training is to be successful, the first step is to encourage the client to see his problem in small units that can be treated through a specific skill training approach. The process of translating from a global to a specific complaint requireds pinpointing the problem in a treatable, solvable way.

Not all older clients accept the rationale of skills training, regardless of how creatively the therapist presents it, nor will they agree initially to cooperate with the procedures. It has been our experience, however, that if the therapist can encourage the client to *experiment,* and the skill decreases aversiveness or increases pleasantness of a given situation, such success is reinforcing. Older clients require a good deal of support and encouragement to follow through on an experimental approach because their behaviors, highly overlearned, produce a tendency to revert to global perceptions and goals rather than focus on specific aspects of the problem situation. In addition, older clients often do not perceive their own power or control in interpersonal situations.

There are any number of skill training areas and techniques that could become the focus of treatment at this point, depending on the nature of the problem. We have found the three described next—assertion, cognitive skills, and communication skills—to be extremely useful because one or more of them will usually be appropriate for the majority of specific problems implicated in depression. Within each of these three skill training areas, there are a number of different approaches that a clinician might want to use, and we have listed several as suggestions. However, we do not see our recommended procedures as exhaustive, and suggest that the reader may wish to refer to other behavioral texts that offer a more comprehensive presentation of recommended approaches. Alternatively, the clinician may wish to apply his own strategies to the areas in question.

The primary point to be remembered here is that the client needs to begin to learn the usefulness of breaking down and pinpointing problems through an experiential process. Any number of skill training procedures could be appropriate for these middle treatment sessions, once the detailed analysis of problem situations has been carried out and the problem operationalized in behavioral terms.

The format used in prior sessions should be followed: set agenda in collaboration with client, elicit feedback as to how procedures are being understood, and review homework at beginning of sessions. Pleasant and Unpleasant Activities Tracking Sheets and Daily Mood Rating Form should remain as basic homework throughout the skill training period. It is usually helpful to reduce the length of the Tracking Sheets to ten pleasant and ten unpleasant activities chosen to be most relevant to each client. (Review Chapter 5 for discussion of how this process is done.)

ASSERTION SKILLS TRAINING

Assertive behavior has been found effective in increasing opportunities for pleasant events and decreasing the number of unpleasant events an individual may experience. It is a practical social skill one can use to more effectively elicit positive (and avoid negative) interpersonal situations. Assertive behavior is the ability to express thoughts and feelings comfortably without infringing upon the rights of others.

Assertive behavior is distinct and different from both aggressive and passive behaviors, and this distinction should be made clear early. While people who respond in an aggressive manner may express themselves clearly, they tend to do so at the expense of others; they rob other people of their own expression by making decisions for them. Passive individuals are frequently, but not always, recipients of other's aggressive behaviors. Non-assertive clients tend to let others make decisions for them and do not openly express their thoughts and feelings.

Both passive and aggressive behaviors can and do lead to many unpleasant events. The passive person may feel frustrated by having a minimal influence on what happens to him, and on how others perceive him. In turn, the aggressive person may be able to get and do what he wants and make feelings clear to others, but in so doing create interpersonal tension experienced as an uncomfortable feeling. Passive and aggressive behaviors are frequently maladaptive. Assertive behavior tends to be the most adaptive.

There are situations in which passive and aggressive behavior may be appropriate. The therapist has the option here of covering these situations when appropriate.

It is not unusual for older adults to find some difficulties in distinguishing between assertive and aggressive behaviors. It is frequently thought that when one asserts oneself, it should be done in a rough and domineering manner. This misconception can be corrected by focusing on the fact that a person does not always have to be expressing a negative thought or feeling, or asking for something, when acting assertively. An expression of positive thoughts and feelings—"I love you"—is also assertion.

Older persons commonly do not act assertively in a number of interpersonal situations. Unpleasant encounters with family members (adult children, spouses, etc.) are perhaps the most frequent examples. The therapist might want to begin assertion training in this area, but he should proceed with caution. Family interpersonal relationships tend to be weighted very heavily in the lives of older adults, and failure of assertive attempts could be detrimental to learning the skill within the time frame of treatment. It is suggested that the therapist start with relationships outside the family or with situations extremely low on a hierarchical list.

ASSERTION TRAINING TECHNIQUES

1. **Pinpoint problem situation(s)** using the problem-solving format introduced earlier. Administration of a brief self-rated assertion questionnaire may be helpful (see Lewinsohn, et al., 1978, pp. 175-177, for such a scale and description of its use).
2. **Employ covert imagery and rehearsal.**
   A. Client verbally describes scene and appropriate assertive response (one client feels good about) to therapist.
   B. Client sits back, and imagines situation, mentally filling in details. Client then vividly imagines self employing assertive response and experiencing a positive consequence of the assertive behavior.
   C. Client repeats Step B, verbally describing the scene and assertive behavior to the therapist.
   D. Therapist and client discuss scene and assertive outcome; they alter details of setting and cueing events in order to build in generality, then look at alternative responses.
   E. Therapist models scene for client, using Step B.
   F. Client tries same scene, accompanying covert imagery with visual description. All these procedures can occur, but may not be required for every client. Therapist's clinical judgment should determine which are necessary. This practice in covert imagery can easily occupy an entire session. It is not unusual for older clients to take more time than younger to create an imagined scene. Plan to spend enough time to make sure the scene is a vivid one.
3. **Suggest homework in covert imagery.** Have the client practice for one to three sessions every day. Scenes should be agreed upon by both client and therapist. Practice should take place at home as

well as in naturally occurring outside settings (banks, buses, markets, etc.). A specific recording form appropriate to the individual client should be developed for this purpose.

4. **Continue practice.** Check client's ability to respond appropriately. Sample at least one response the client used in each of the assigned scenes. Reinforce appropriate responses and/or make necessary corrections. Some clients may have difficulty with imagery, or for other reasons may not need the covert procedure described above. In such case, the therapist may wish to start role playing procedures directly.

5. **Role playing and rehearsal.** Particular assertive response to be tried in vivo.
   A. Following covert practice series, have client play self, therapist play significant other.
   B. Discuss details of client's assertive response. Suggest alternative adaptive responses, and repeat Step A.
   C. Discuss assertive response with client. Make revisions if necessary, and reverse roles, with therapist modeling assertion for client.
   D. Have client repeat assertive response; discuss, making sure client feels outcome is pleasant. Client should try assertive responses in vivo at least once before next session. Help client plan good potential settings in which to try out the behavior.

6. **Suggest readings for additional information.**
   Alberti, R., & Emmons, M. *Your Perfect Right* (2nd ed.). San Luis Obispo, CA: Impact, 1974.
   Fensterheim, H., & Baer, J. *Don't Say Yes When You Want to Say No.* New York: Dell, 1975.
   Gombrill, E., & Richey, C. *It's Up to You: The Development of Assertive Social Skills.* Millbrae, CA: Les Femmes, 1976.

COGNITIVE SKILLS TRAINING

Often when persons are depressed, they experience an elevated frequency of negative thoughts. These are cognitions about self, other people, and situations or events which are irrational, pessimistic, and self defeating. These negative thoughts may or may not be verbalized by the client, but are energy consuming and contribute to feelings of depression. Such thoughts have two important implications for treatment: (1) they may constitute a class of unpleasant events in and of themselves, and (2) they may interfere with more constructive problem solving approaches designed to increase pleasant events and decrease unpleasant events.

Negative Thoughts Found Frequently in Older Persons

Negative thoughts must first be identified and labeled as such before clients can deal constructively with them. We have observed several content areas of negative thinking expressed by a number of different clients. While some of these reflect valid concerns, they can become unrealistically negative and maladaptive.

1. **Preoccupation with physical problems** is often evident. Some older clients become obsessed with the limiting consequences of physical disabilities. Because their health does not meet standards of a younger age, they believe they can no longer engage in pleasant activities, or that life is not worth living.

2. **Thoughts about the past become problematic** when persons ruminate obsessively about past mistakes or failure to achieve goals. Some clients become unable to interpret the past in more adaptive ways and to accept the constraints operating on their lives.

3. **Disappointments with adult children** may become an example of negative thinking, especially when clients blame themselves for mistakes made.

4. **The death of family members and friends** may also be perceived in an overly negative way. A tendency to focus on prior conflicts or problems in a relationship and unresolved feelings of guilt and anger may be maladaptive; also, a client may express the feeling that life cannot be meaningful without the deceased person.

5. **Appearance changes with age** are felt by some older persons to render them unattractive and unappealing to others. This reduces their social stimulus value, and consequently their feelings of self-esteem or self-worth.

6. **Loss of social roles** causes some older persons to experience a sense of uselessness. To believe that loss of work or of parenting role removes all opportunities to demonstrate competence and mastery is negative thinking.

7. **The need to care for an ill or impaired spouse or family member** may create for many older persons the feeling that they face overwhelming responsibilities with no free time, and therefore are unable to pursue pleasant events.

8. **Historical and social changes** are sometimes perceived by the older client in a negative way, a view which contributes to feelings of hopelessness about the future of the world and humanity in general.

9. **Intense fear of low probability events—crime or accidents—** can prevent the older person from engaging in pleasant events or severely limit mobility through fear of using public transportation or going out alone.

10. **Concern that sexual performance will not match that of youth** can prevent or discourage engagement in sexual activities.

Steps in Changing Negative Thoughts in Older Persons

1. Identify negative thoughts as such.
2. Target specific negative thoughts to be changed.
3. Decide which technique is most appropriate.
4. Present technique to client and assign tasks as homework.
5. After the client has had an opportunity to practice the technique, discuss its effectiveness with the client.
6. If effectiveness is unsatisfactory, apply alternative techniques until client has some success gaining control over negative thoughts.

(An excellent resource for both therapist and client to consider reading on these points is Lewinsohn et al., 1978, pp. 217-239).

COGNITIVE SKILLS TECHNIQUES

Once the client has recognized negative thinking as a problem, standard techniques for reducing negative thoughts and increasing positive thoughts can be tailored to the specific needs of the person.

1. **Decrease negative thoughts**
   A. Thought stopping—each time the negative thought occurs, verbally or mentally shout "Stop!"; immediately think of something else.
   B. Pair an aversive stimulus with targeted negative thought when it occurs (wear rubber band around wrist and snap it whenever negative thought emerges).
   C. Blow-up technique—exaggerate qualities or consequences of disturbing thought to a point of absurdity.
   D. Worry time—set aside a period of time to do nothing except obsess about a disturbing thought; allow no other activity except worrying.

2. **Increase positive thoughts**
   A. Thought substitution—(1) replace negative thought with a pre-planned positive thought, or (2) modify an irrational or extreme position thought to a rational or moderate position thought (a technique to encourage more constructive reevaluation of a situation or problem).
   B. "Premacking"—pair a pleasant thought or positive self statement with a frequently occurring event such as brushing teeth.
   C. "Priming"—prepare list of positive self statements (write them on index cards so they will always be available to client). Instruct client to read these and reflect on positive traits several times a day.
   D. Self reinforcement—instruct client to reward self for increasing positive thoughts.

3. Suggest readings for additional information:
  Burns, D. *Feeling Good.* New York: Morrow, 1980.
  Ellis, A., & Harper, R. *A Guide to Rational Living.* North
    Hollywood, CA: Wilshire Book Co., 1973.
  Mahoney, M.J., & Thoreson, C. *Self-Control: Power to the
    Person.* Monterey, CA: Brooks/Cole, 1974.

COMMUNICATION SKILLS TRAINING

The development of effective communication skills is often a key element in treatment of depression. Depressed people are restricted in their range of social opportunities, have difficulty initiating new relationships, and frequently are unaware of the impact they have on others. These three components will be addressed in this section. Other important communication skills are covered in the Assertiveness Training section; the two may be used in conjunction or separately, according to client needs.

Because this is such a broad area for intervention, and often a sensitive one for clients (who are apt to feel criticized when this topic is first introduced), a good deal of therapist skill is needed to effectively bring about change. Workable target behaviors need to be selected carefully, and flexibility in use of techniques and creation of homework assignments is critical. While most clients are willing to expand opportunities for social outlets (the first area discussed below) many are reluctant to initiate new social relationships and/or critically evaluate their impact on others. The latter two issues often reflect longstanding personality styles. Unless the client is enthusiastic about tackling these, the therapist probably should not press too hard. While certain concrete behaviors may change, often more extensive therapy is required to modify aspects of personality style. For many older clients, these areas will be beyond the scope of this treatment procedure, and a referral for additional therapy may be indicated. How far to go with this is a matter of client motivation and clinical judgment.

COMMUNICATION SKILLS TECHNIQUES

Expanding Opportunities for Social Outlets

Depressed older people are often particularly restricted in range of social opportunities because of health and mobility problems, financial limitations, and narrowing of social networks through death or separation from significant others. It is crucial for the therapist to explore the client's social environment and to be conversant with resources available in the client's community (senior call lines, senior specialists, Area Administrations on Aging, senior centers, and gerontology centers).

The client may not be aware of available activities in which he can participate despite realistic limitations. In addition, depressed people typically have an unreasonably low appraisal of their ability to participate in social systems. This promotes withdrawal from social environments which could be supportive, thereby reinforcing negative feelings about themselves.

A detailed analysis of a client's interests, hobbies, abilities, and desire for social interaction is needed before proceeding with communication skill training. The analysis should begin by assessing physical mobility and financial limitations through observation and discussion with the client. Information about interests, hobbies, and desired amount of social interaction can be learned from study of accumulated Pleasant Activities Tracking Sheets. These data should help identify specific social activities available to the client.

At this point, although the therapist may desire to proceed by simply listing available resources, expecting the client to proceed on his own, a step-by-step approach has been found more effective with older depressed clients. The first step may be to have the client select a single activity he is interested in exploring; the next step would be to have him gather specific information regarding this activity (by phone; by requesting a brochure from the appropriate source); and finally, the therapist would assign the client the task of making an initial visit in person. Occasionally it may be necessary for the therapist to accompany the client on the initial visit; once done with therapist guidance, the client will be more likely to be able to continue this process to explore other social environments and opportunities.

Initiating Social Relationships

It is usually not sufficient to introduce a client to new environments. A depressed person typically will experience much anxiety in a new situation and be unable to make use of the opportunity without training in techniques for initiating and maintaining social relationships. Learning techniques for "breaking the ice" can be very helpful at this point; a good resource for this kind of skill training is *When I Say No, I Feel Guilty* by Manuel Smith. Techniques covered include self disclosure, eliciting feedback from others, and eliciting personal information from others. The therapist would want to role play these techniques with the client prior to his participation in an actual situation.

Role reversal and therapist modeling of the various kinds of responses have proved helpful with older clients. The therapist may also need to address the client's negative self statements which could inhibit enjoyment of social interaction (see Cognitive Skills Techniques section).

Impact on Others

Older depressed people are frequently unaware of their impact on others, or have inaccurate perceptions. The therapist should assess the client's willingness to explore verbal and nonverbal behaviors that are contributing to aversive responses from others before proceeding to point them out to the client. These behaviors could be determined by discussion with the client, viewing videotapes, or by therapist assessment of an obvious block to development of satisfying personal relationships. Verbal behaviors could include speech rate (slow), latency of response, number of positive statements, reinforcement of other's behavior, depressive talk (complaints); nonverbal behaviors would include dress, grooming, warmth, smiles, facial expressions, gestures, eye contact, and posture. The client's reaction to this issue of impact on others should be discussed, and together client and therapist should select one or two target behaviors to be improved. This step requires considerable tact and clinical skill; the client should feel supported rather than criticized through this procedure.

It is important for the therapist to communicate (1) that these behaviors are habits of long duration, and (2) that the therapist's aim is to set in motion a process which the client can continue beyond treatment. For more extensive behavior change along these lines, additional treatment in a group setting or experiences in another supportive environment may be necessary.

Once target behaviors have been identified and the goals set, specific assignments can be made. The client may be assigned daily practice sessions (rehearsing facial expressions and postures by himself with the aid of a mirror, or increasing eye contact and positive statements with a supportive friend or relative).

Therapy time itself may be structured to practice the behavior receiving attention (decrease "depressive talk" by requesting that the client converse with therapist on another topic the client finds enjoyable). Videotapes can be viewed with client to monitor progress. A number of self help books that deal with client's specific needs could be recommended. These include:

Smith, M. *When I Say No, I Feel Guilty.* New York: Bantam Books, 1975.

Zimbardo, P. *Shyness: What It Is; What To Do About It.* Reading, MA: Addison-Wesley, 1975.

Zunin, L., & Zunin, N. *Contact: The First Four Minutes.* New York: Ballantine Books, 1972.

References

Bandura, A., Self-efficacy: Toward unifying theory of behavioral change. *Psychological Review,* 1977, *84,* 191-215.

Beck, A., Rush, J., Shaw, B., & Emery, G. *Cognitive therapy of depression.* New York: Guilford Press, 1979.

Beck, A.T., Ward, C.H., Mendelson, M., Mock, J.E., & Erbaugh, J. An inventory for measuring depression. *Archives of General Psychiatry,* 1961, *4,* 561-571.

Berger, R., & Rose, S. Interpersonal skill training with institutionalized elderly patients. *Journal of Gerontology,* 1977, *32,* 346-353.

Botwinick, J. *Aging and behavior* (2nd ed.). New York: Springer, 1978.

Brown, R.A., & Lewinsohn, P. *A psychoeducational approach to the treatment of depression: Comparison of group, individual and minimal contact procedures.* University of Oregon, unpublished manuscript, 1980.

Butler, R. & Lewis, M. *Aging and mental health* (2nd ed.). St. Louis: Mosby, 1977.

Derogatis, L., Lipman, R., & Covi, L. The SCL-90: An outpatient psychiatric rating scale. *Psychopharmacology Bulletin,* 1973, *9,* 13-28.

Dessonville, C., Gallagher, D., Thompson, L., & Finnel, K. *Depressive symptomatology in normal and depressed elderly.* Paper presented at the American Psychological Association meetings, Montreal, August, 1980.

Endicott, J., & Spitzer, R.L. A diagnostic interview: The schedule for affective disorders and schizophrenia. *Archives of General Psychiatry,* 1978, *35,* 837-844.

Epstein, L.J. Symposium on age differentiation in depressive illness: Depression in the elderly. *Journal of Gerontology,* 1976, *31,* 278-282.

Feighner, J., Robins, E., & Guze, S. Diagnostic criteria for use in psychiatric research. *Archives of General Psychiatry,* 1972, *26,* 57-63.

Folstein, M., Folstein, S., & McHugh, P. "Mini-Mental State"—A practical method for grading the cognitive state of patients for the clinician. *Journal of Psychiatric Research,* 1975, *12,* 189-198.

Fuchs, C., & Rehm, L. A self-control behavior therapy program for depression. *Journal of Consulting and Clinical Psychology,* 1977, *45,* 206-215.

Gallagher, D. Behavioral group therapy with elderly depressives: An experimental study. In D. Upper & S. Ross (Eds.), *Behavioral group therapy.* Champaign, Ill.: Research Press, 1981 (in press).

Gallagher, D., & Frankel, A.S. Depression in (an) older adult(s): A moderate structuralist viewpoint. *Psychotherapy: Theory, Research and Practice,* 1980, *17,* 101-104.

Gallagher, D., & Nies, G. *Reliability of the Beck Depression Inventory with older adults.* University of Southern California, unpublished manuscript, 1981.

Gallagher, D., & Thompson, L. *Cognitive therapy for depression in the elderly: Problems and issues.* Paper presented at symposium on Depression in the Elderly: Causes, Care, Consequences, sponsored by the Center on Aging and Health, Case Western Reserve University, Cleveland, Ohio, October, 1980.

Gallagher, D., Thompson, L., & Stone, V. *Relationship between Beck Depression Inventory scores and clinical diagnosis of depression in the elderly.* University of Southern California, unpublished manuscript, 1981.

Garfield, S.L., & Bergin, A.E. *Handbook of psychotherapy and behavior change: An empirical analysis* (2nd ed.). New York: Wiley, 1978.

Gerner, R. *Depression in the elderly.* In O. Kaplan (Ed.), *Psychopathology of aging.* New York: Academic Press, 1979.

Gurland, B. The comparative frequency of depression in various adult age groups. *Journal of Gerontology,* 1976, *31,* 283-292.

Hamilton, M. A rating scale for depression. *Journal of Neurology, Neurosurgery, and Psychiatry,* 1960, *23,* 56-62.

Hamilton, M. Development of a rating scale for primary depressive illness. *British Journal of Social and Clinical Psychology,* 1967, *6,* 278-296.

Harmatz, J., & Shader, R. Psychopharmacologic investigations in healthy elderly volunteers: MMPI depression scale. *Journal of American Geriatrics Society,* 1975, *23,* 350-354.

Hathaway, S.R., & McKinley, J.C. *The Minnesota Multiphasic Personality Inventory Manual.* Minneapolis: University of Minnesota Press, 1943.

Hedlund, B., & Gilewski, M. *Development of Pleasant and Unpleasant Events Schedules for Older Adults: A validation study of short forms for use with elderly individuals.* Unpublished manuscript, University of Southern California, 1980.

Kahn, R.L., Goldfarb, A.I., Pollack, M., & Peck, A. A brief objective measure for the determination of mental status of the aged. *American Journal of Psychiatry,* 1960, *117,* 326-328.

Kanfer, F. & Saslow, G. Behavioral diagnosis. In C. Franks (Ed.), *Behavioral therapy: Appraisal & status.* New York: McGraw-Hill, 1969.

Klerman, G., Rounsaville, B., & Chevron, E. *Manual for short-term interpersonal psychotherapy (IPT) of depression.* Yale University School of Medicine; unpublished data, April, 1979.

Kogan, N., & Wallach, M. *Risk taking: A study in cognition and personality.* New York: Holt, Rinehart & Winston, 1964.

Kovacs, M., Rush, J., Beck, A.T., & Hollon, S. Depressed outpatients treated with cognitive therapy or pharmacotherapy: A one-year follow-up. *Archives of General Psychiatry,* 1981, *38,* 33-39.

Knight, B. Psychotherapy and behavior changes with the non-institutionalized aged. *International Journal of Aging and Human Development,* 1978-79, *9,* 221-236.

LaRue, A., Bank, L., Jarvik, L., & Hetland, M. Health in old age: How do physicians' ratings and self-ratings compare? *Journal of Gerontology, 1979, 34,* 687-691.

Levy, S., Derogatis, L., Gallagher, D., & Gatz, M. Intervention with older adults and the evaluation of outcome. In L. Poon (Ed.), *Aging in the 1980's.* Washington, D.C., American Psychological Association, 1980.

Lewinsohn, P. A behavioral approach to depression. In R. Friedman & M. Katz (Eds.), *The Psychology of depression: contemporary theory and research.* New York: Wiley, 1974.

Lewinsohn, P. Engagement in pleasant activities and depression level. *Journal of Abnormal Psychology,* 1975, *83,* 729-731.

Lewinsohn, P., & Grosscup, S. *Decreasing unpleasant events and increasing pleasant events: A treatment manual for depression.* Unpublished manuscript, University of Oregon, 1978.

Lewinsohn, P., Sullivan, J.M., & Grosscup, S. *Changing reinforcing events: An approach to the treatment of depression.* University of Oregon, unpublished manuscript, 1980.

Lewinsohn, P., Munoz, R., Youngren, M.A., & Zeiss, A. *Control your depression.* Englewood Cliffs, N.J.: Prentice-Hall, 1978.

McGarvey, B., Gallagher, D., & Thompson, L. Reliability and factor structure of the Zung Self-Rating Depression Scale in three age groups. *Journal of Gerontology,* in press.

Pfeiffer, E. A short portable mental status questionnaire for the assessment of organic brain deficit in elderly patients. *Journal of the American Geriatrics Society,* 1975, *10,* 433-441.

Popkin, S., Gallagher, D., Thompson, L., & Moore, M. *Memory complaint and performance in normal and depressed older adults.* Paper presented at the American Psychological Association meetings, Montreal, August, 1980.

Raskin, A., & Jarvik, L. *Psychiatric symptoms and cognitive loss in the elderly.* Washington, D.C.: Hemisphere, 1979.

Redick, R., & Taube, C. Demography and mental health care of the aged. In J. Birren & R. Sloan (Eds.), *Handbook of mental health and aging.* Englewood Cliffs: Prentice-Hall, 1980.

Rehm, L. A self-control model of depression. *Behavior Therapy,* 1977, *8,* 787-804.

Rimm, D.C., & Masters, J.C. *Behavior therapy: Techniques and empirical findings.* New York: Academic Press, 1974.

Rush, J., Beck, A., Kovacs, M., & Hallon, S. Comparative efficacy of cognitive therapy and imipramine in the treatment of depressed outpatients. *Cognitive Therapy and Research,* 1977, *1,* 17-37.

Salzman, C. & Shader, R. Clinical evaluation of depression in the elderly. In A. Raskin & L. Jarvik (Eds.), *Psychiatric symptoms and cognitive loss in the elderly.* Washington, D.C.: Hemisphere, 1979.

Seigal, S. *Non-parametric statistics for the behavioral sciences.* New York: McGraw-Hill, 1956.

Silverman, C. *The epidemiology of depression.* Baltimore: Johns Hopkins, 1968.

Spitzer, R.L., Endicott, J., & Robins, E. Research diagnostic criteria: Rationale and reliability. *Archives of General Psychiatry,* 1978, *35,* 773-782.

Thompson, L., & Gallagher, D. *Psychotherapy for depression in the elderly.* Progress Report, NIMH Grant #R01 - 32157, prepared October, 1980.

Weissman, M., Klerman, G., Prusoff, B., Scholomskas, M., & Padian, N. Depressed outpatients: Results one year after treatment with drugs and/or interpersonal psychotherapy. *Archives of General Psychiatry,* 1981, *38,* 51-55.

Wolberg, L.R. *Short-term psychotherapy.* New York: Grune & Stratton, 1965.

Zarit, S. *Aging and mental disorders.* New York: The Free Press, 1980.

Zung, W. A self-rating depression scale. *Archives of General Psychiatry,* 1965, *12,* 63-70.

Zung, W. Depression in the normal aged. *Psychosomatics,* 1967, *8,* 287-291.

Appendices

Subject # _____

Interview # _____

Date _____

BECK INVENTORY*

Instructions: This questionnaire contains groups of statements. Please read each group of statements carefully. Then pick out the one statement in each group which best describes the way you have been feeling *during the past week, including today!* Circle the number beside the statement you have chosen.

Be sure to read all the statements in each group before making your choice.

---

1. 0 I do not feel sad.
    1 I feel sad.
    2 I am sad all the time and I can't snap out of it.
    3 I am so sad or unhappy that I can't stand it.

---

2. 0 I am not particularly discouraged about the future.
    1 I feel discouraged about the future.
    2 I feel I have nothing to look forward to.
    3 I feel the future is hopeless and that things cannot improve.

---

3. 0 I do not feel like a failure.
    1 I feel I have failed more than the average person.
    2 As I look back on my life, all I can see is a lot of failure.
    3 I feel I am a complete failure as a person.

---

*©1978 by Aaron T. Beck, M.D. The authors wish to thank Aaron T. Beck, M.D., for granting permission to reprint the Beck Depression Inventory.

4. 0 I get as much satisfaction out of things as I used to.
    1 I don't enjoy things the way I used to.
    2 I don't get real satisfaction out of anything anymore.
    3 I am dissatisfied or bored with everything.

5. 0 I don't feel particularly guilty.
    1 I feel guilty a good part of the time.
    2 I feel quite guilty most of the time.
    3 I feel guilty all of the time.

6. 0 I don't feel I am being punished.
    1 I feel I may be punished.
    2 I expect to be punished.
    3 I feel I am being punished.

7. 0 I don't feel disappointed in myself.
    1 I am disappointed in myself.
    2 I am disgusted with myself.
    3 I hate myself.

8. 0 I don't feel I am any worse than anyone else.
    1 I am critical of myself for my weaknesses or faults.
    2 I blame myself all the time for my faults.
    3 I blame myself for everything bad that happens.

9. 0 I don't have thoughts of killing myself.
    1 I have thoughts of killing myself, but I would not carry them out.
    2 I would like to kill myself.
    3 I would kill myself if I had the chance.

10. 0 I don't cry any more than usual.
    1 I cry more now than I used to.
    2 I cry all the time now.
    3 I used to be able to cry, but now I can't cry even though I want to.

11. 0 I am no more irritated now than I ever am.
    1 I get annoyed or irritated more easily than I used to.
    2 I feel irritated all the time now.
    3 I don't get irritated at all by the things that used to irritate me.

12. 0 I have not lost interest in other people.
    1 I am less interested in other people than I used to be.
    2 I have lost most of my interest in other people.
    3 I have lost all of my interest in other people.

13. 0 I make decisions about as well as I ever could.
    1 I put off making decisions more than I used to.
    2 I have greater difficulty in making decisions than before.
    3 I can't make decisions at all anymore.

14. 0 I don't feel I look worse than I used to.
    1 I am worried that I am looking old or unattractive.
    2 I feel that there are permanent changes in my appearance that make me look unattractive.
    3 I believe that I look ugly.

15. 0 I can work about as well as I used to.
    1 It takes an extra effort to get started at doing something.
    2 I have to push myself very hard to do anything.
    3 I can't do any work at all.

16. 0 I can sleep as well as usual.
    1 I don't sleep as well as I used to.
    2 I wake up 1-2 hours earlier than usual and find it hard to get back to sleep.
    3 I wake up several hours earlier than I used to and cannot get back to sleep.

17. 0 I don't get more tired than usual.
     1 I get tired more easily than I used to.
     2 I get tired from doing almost nothing.
     3 I am too tired to do anything.

18. 0 My appetite is no worse than usual.
     1 My appetite is not as good as it used to be.
     2 My appetite is much worse now.
     3 I have no appetite at all anymore.

19. 0 I haven't lost much weight, if any, lately.
     1 I have lost more than 5 pounds.
     2 I have lost more than 10 pounds.
     3 I have lost more than 15 pounds.

20. 0 I am no more worried about my health than usual.
     1 I am worried about physical problems such as aches and pains or upset stomach or constipation.
     2 I am very much worried about my physical problems and it's hard to think of much else.
     3 I am so worried about my physical problems that I cannot think about anything else.

21. 0 I have not noticed any recent change in my interest in sex.
     1 I am much less interested in sex than I used to be.
     2 I am much less interested in sex now.
     3 I have lost interest in sex completely.

22. I am purposely trying to lose weight by eating less:

    _____ Yes   _____ No

APPENDIX 2

CONTROL YOUR DEPRESSION

We have prepared this description of what depression is and how behavioral therapy goes about treating depression so you can understand what your therapist's approach will be. Please read it over carefully and note wherever you have questions. You should be prepared to raise these questions and any other issues that occur to you as you read this when you come in for your next appointment.

Persons who are depressed tend to engage in only a small number of activities which are experienced as enjoyable by them. We know this because prior research has demonstrated a relationship between rate of engagement in pleasant activities and mood level. This means that people feel best when experiencing an optimal rate of engagement in pleasant activities.

Research has also demonstrated a relationship between rate of occurrence of unpleasant events and mood level. The fact that there is a strong association between your feelings and how often you engage in pleasant and unpleasant activities suggests a novel treatment approach for coping with depression.

The major goals of this treatment program are to help you to:

1. Reduce the number of unpleasant events that happen to you;

2. Lessen the intensity of how bad you feel when unpleasant things do happen;

3. Increase the number of pleasant activities you experience;

4. Enhance the enjoyment of pleasant activities; and

5. Apply the techniques and skills learned in the therapy sessions to a wide variety of situations to facilitate your ability to maintain an improved mood level and to prevent future depression.

Everyone has times of feeling sad or blue. People often refer to these feelings by saying they are "depressed". However, we are restricting our discussion of depression to something one experiences or feels for a period of time. Sometimes the beginning of a period of depression is clear and dramatic and is related to a specific event. More often, though, there is no easily identified event that precedes depression. Rather, depression is experienced from time to time without any obvious explanation.

Symptoms of Depression

The depressive syndrome is a collection of rather specific feelings and behaviors that have been found to be characteristic of depressed persons as a group. It is important to recognize that there are large individual differences as to which of these feelings or behaviors are experienced, and to what extent they are experienced. The following are characteristics of the depressive syndrome:

1. **Dysphoria.** By dysphoria, we mean an unpleasant feeling state. Dysphoria is the opposite of euphoria (feeling very happy). People who are depressed frequently say they feel very sad, blue, hopeless, or "down" much of the time.

2. **Problems Interacting with Other People.** Many depressed persons express concern about their interpersonal relationships. This concern may be expressed in a variety of ways. Some individuals are very unhappy or dissatisfied with their marital relationships or with other close, ongoing relationships. Others feel uncomfortable and anxious when they are with other people, especially in groups.

3. **Guilt.** Some depressed persons express feelings of guilt and believe they deserve to be punished for their "badness" or "sinfulness." Others feel guilt because of their failure—real or imagined—to assume responsibilities in their family lives or jobs.

4. **Feeling Burdened.** Some individuals do not feel at all responsible for their own depression; instead they blame their distress on external causes. Such persons typically complain that others are always putting excessive demands upon them.

5. **Physical Problems.** A common problem among depressed individuals is having low energy or feelings of fatigue for long periods of time with no obvious explanation. Sleep disturbance of some kind also is common. In addition, depressed persons sometimes experience a loss of appetite and may show a weight loss. Other physical problems associated with depression include increased frequency and severity of headaches, stomachaches, intestinal difficulties, and reduced interest in sexual activity.

6. **Low Level of Activity.** This is a particularly important symptom of depression. Depressed persons do considerably less overall when they are depressed. Sometimes a depressed person's typical day consists largely of "sitting around and doing nothing" or engaging in mostly passive, solitary activities like watching television, eating, or napping. Going to work or taking care of daily household chores may seem to require an almost overwhelming amount of effort.

Often the depressed person feels unmotivated to engage in hobbies or other activities that used to be enjoyable or satisfying.

Such activities no longer appeal to the person and seem like "just another chore" that would require too much effort.

Again, it is important to remember that these features of the depressive syndrome are characteristic of depressed persons as a group; the depressed individual typically experiences only some of them. For example, a person's feelings may be dominated by sadness and hopelessness without experiencing any guilt. Or someone may feel "slowed-down" and fatigued without having headaches.

The fact that depressed individuals are not as active as they once were suggests a new approach for treating depression and new ways in which the depressed individual can help himself. Therapists who treat patients with complaints of depression are becoming increasingly concerned with improving the overall activity rate of the patient by increasing pleasant events and decreasing unpleasant events.

Understanding Depression

It is useful to look at how feelings of depression begin. Except when we are sleeping, we are continuously interacting with our environment. Whether we are watching television, typing a report, talking to a salesperson, interacting with our children or spouse, talking to someone on the telephone, or just sitting and ruminating about something from the past, we are always doing something. Our interaction with our environment is continous and reciprocal.

In a general way we can put our interactions into categories— those that lead to positive outcomes (you finish an art project and your daughter compliments you on it), those that have neutral outcomes (you drive to a supermarket in the morning), and those that have negative outcomes (being criticized by someone who is important to you). When too few of our interactions have positive outcomes and when too many of them have negative outcomes, we start feeling depressed.

Obviously, not all of our interactions can be expected to lead to positive consequences; neither is it reasonable to expect that none of our actions will lead to negative consequences. Nevertheless, without a reasonable balance between positive and negative outcomes, anybody is going to feel depressed.

When too many of our interactions lack positive outcomes or are associated with negative outcomes, a vicious cycle can begin where we engage in fewer and fewer activities. This greatly reduces the potential for positive outcomes, so we feel even more depressed and consequently become even less active. There are several ways this cycle can get started.

1. Interactions that have been a source of positive outcomes for you in the past are no longer available. For example, a loved one dies, or a close friend moves to a retirement community several hundred miles away.

2. You may lack the skill to elicit positive outcomes from your interactions. For example, you may feel inadequate or uncomfortable making conversation with new acquaintances at a party.

3. The pool of potentially enjoyable activities may be considerably reduced. For example, financial restrictions based on a retirement income may limit activities.

Once the vicious cycle is established, the depression may be strengthened if "talking depression" leads to positive outcomes with the environment. For example, take the case of Mary, a 68-year-old widow with one daughter who lives in a distant area of the city. When Mary's husband first died, her daughter, Suellen, was an important source of emotional support and a frequent companion. About a year ago, Suellen got a new job which requires much of her time and energy. Now she spends considerably less time with Mary, and the only time she really appears interested in what her mother is saying is when Mary talks about her feelings of depression and thoughts of suicide. Unwittingly, Mary has found a key to obtaining Suellen's attention. We would predict that the frequency with which she would report her symptoms to Suellen will increase.

What to Do

The major goal of this treatment is for you to learn new ways (or relearn old ways) of obtaining positive outcomes from the environment by engaging in more pleasant activities. Our research shows that for most people, increasing pleasant events and decreasing unpleasant events reverses the vicious cycle described above and reduces or stops feelings of depression.

Of course, changing your activity pattern is a gradual process where you and your therapist will work together. First, you will be asked to complete daily activity charts and mood ratings. This *self-observation* will help both you and your therapist set appropriate goals and evaluate your progress. A second important part of this program is *relaxation training*. Learning to get relaxed is a skill which can be used in many different situations to increase the pleasantness and/or decrease the unpleasantness of certain events. You will also work on *specific skill deficits* which may have prevented you from engaging in particular pleasant activities. These will vary widely from person to person, but might include skills such as assertion training or communication and listening skills training. Throughout every phase of treatment we will focus on reducing or eliminating feelings of depression by increasing pleasant events and decreasing unpleasant events.

There are several general strategies your therapist will discuss which may facilitate your efforts to change:

1. Self-reinforcement: rewarding yourself for accomplishing what you have decided to change.

2. Step-by-step change: slow, deliberate change in an area chosen by the individual. In its most concrete form, gradual change means increasing or decreasing by very small steps the amount of time or the number of times that you perform the target behavior. Self-reward for each successful step is part of this process.

3. Modeling: learning by observing others. You can use people whom you like (public figures, or fictional characters) as models of the kind of behavior you want to develop and use.

4. Self-observation: noticing and keeping written records of your behavior and feelings.

In summary, this approach to treating depression is based on research which shows that feelings of depression are associated with a low rate of pleasant activities resulting in positive outcomes and/or a high rate of unpleasant activities resulting in negative outcomes. Treatment will last a total of 16 sessions. During these 16 sessions you and your therapist will work together, using a variety of techniques, in order for you to learn how to change your activity pattern. In additon, you are expected to complete homework assignments each week which are related to the issues discussed in therapy. Your therapist will help you identify problem areas, set realistic goals, and learn new skills (or relearn old skills) which will help you attain these goals. By increasing the pleasant activities and decreasing unpleasant activities, you will learn a new way of controlling feelings of depression.

APPENDIX 3

THERAPIST'S PROGRESS NOTES

Client _____

Date _____

1. BDI score _____
2. Review homework (check) _____
3. Themes discussed in session

Content	**Intervention (what did you do?)**
A. _____	A. _____
B. _____	B. _____
C. _____	C. _____
D. _____	D. _____
E. _____	E. _____
F. _____	F. _____
G. _____	G. _____
H. _____	H. _____

4. Was homework assigned for next time?   Yes _____   No _____
   Describe homework:

   _____
   _____
   _____

5. Was session conduct different from approach used with younger person? How?

   _____
   _____
   _____

6. Client's progress: _____
   _____

7. How did you feel at end of session (frustrated, satisfied, confident, depressed, etc.)? _____

   _____

APPENDIX 4

OLDER PERSONS' PLEASANT EVENTS SCHEDULE

	How often have these events occurred in your life in the past month?	How pleasant is each event? *Rate whether or not event occurred in the past month.*	
	0 = Not at all 1 = 1-6 times 2 = 7 times or more	0 = Not pleasant 1 = Somewhat pleasant 2 = Very pleasant	
	Circle one number	**Circle one number**	**Cross product**
1. Looking at clouds	0 1 2	0 1 2	
2. Having people show an interest in what I say	0 1 2	0 1 2	
3. Being with friends	0 1 2	0 1 2	
4. Seeing beautiful scenery	0 1 2	0 1 2	
5. Having a frank and open conversation	0 1 2	0 1 2	
6. Having coffee, tea, etc. with friends	0 1 2	0 1 2	
7. Thinking about pleasant memories	0 1 2	0 1 2	
8. Kissing, touching/showing affection	0 1 2	0 1 2	
9. Doing a job well	0 1 2	0 1 2	
10. Seeing good things happen to family or friends	0 1 2	0 1 2	
11. Saying something clearly	0 1 2	0 1 2	
12. Complimenting/praising someone	0 1 2	0 1 2	
13. Amusing people	0 1 2	0 1 2	
14. Being with someone I love	0 1 2	0 1 2	
15. Making a new friend	0 1 2	0 1 2	
16. Being complimented or told I have done something well	0 1 2	0 1 2	
17. Expressing my love to someone	0 1 2	0 1 2	
18. Helping someone	0 1 2	0 1 2	

	FREQUENCY			PLEASANTNESS			

	0 = Not at all
	1 = 1-6 times
	2 = 7 times
	  or more
				0 = Not pleasant
				1 = Somewhat
				  pleasant
				2 = Very pleasant			

	Circle one number			Circle one number			Cross product
19. Listening to sounds of nature	0	1	2	0	1	2	
20. Meeting someone new of the same sex	0	1	2	0	1	2	
21. Planning trips or vacations	0	1	2	0	1	2	
22. Being praised by people I admire	0	1	2	0	1	2	
23. Doing a project my own way	0	1	2	0	1	2	
24. Being told I am needed	0	1	2	0	1	2	
25. Being loved	0	1	2	0	1	2	
26. Listening to music	0	1	2	0	1	2	
27. Completing a difficult task	0	1	2	0	1	2	
28. Having an original idea	0	1	2	0	1	2	
29. Seeing or smelling a flower or plant	0	1	2	0	1	2	
30. Being asked for help or advice	0	1	2	0	1	2	
31. Thinking about myself	0	1	2	0	1	2	
32. Being with happy people	0	1	2	0	1	2	
33. Looking at the stars or moon	0	1	2	0	1	2	
34. Giving advice to others based on past experience	0	1	2	0	1	2	
35. Watching a sunset	0	1	2	0	1	2	
36. Reading literature	0	1	2	0	1	2	
37. Listening to the birds sing	0	1	2	0	1	2	
38. Reading magazines	0	1	2	0	1	2	
39. Being needed	0	1	2	0	1	2	
40. Having a clean house	0	1	2	0	1	2	
41. Having a daily plan	0	1	2	0	1	2	
42. Shopping	0	1	2	0	1	2	
43. Smiling at people	0	1	2	0	1	2	
44. Planning or organizing something	0	1	2	0	1	2	
45. Meditating	0	1	2	0	1	2	

	FREQUENCY	PLEASANTNESS	

	0 = Not at all
	1 = 1-6 times
	2 = 7 times
	   or more
		0 = Not pleasant
		1 = Somewhat
		   pleasant
		2 = Very pleasant	

	Circle one number	Circle one number	Cross product
46. Solving a problem, puzzle, crossword	0 1 2	0 1 2	
47. Getting out of the city (mountains, seashore, desert)	0 1 2	0 1 2	
48. Exploring new areas	0 1 2	0 1 2	
49. Visiting a museum	0 1 2	0 1 2	
50. Doing volunteer work	0 1 2	0 1 2	
51. Collecting recipes	0 1 2	0 1 2	
52. Working on a community project	0 1 2	0 1 2	
53. Baking because I feel creative	0 1 2	0 1 2	
54. Listening to classical music	0 1 2	0 1 2	
55. Bargain hunting	0 1 2	0 1 2	
56. Arranging flowers	0 1 2	0 1 2	
57. Creative crafts	0 1 2	0 1 2	
58. Shopping for a new outfit	0 1 2	0 1 2	
59. Thinking about something good in the future	0 1 2	0 1 2	
60. Thinking about people I like	0 1 2	0 1 2	
61. Having peace and quiet	0 1 2	0 1 2	
62. Feeling a divine presence	0 1 2	0 1 2	
63. Having spare time	0 1 2	0 1 2	
64. Being near sand, grass, a stream	0 1 2	0 1 2	
65. Going to church	0 1 2	0 1 2	
66. Taking inventory of my life	0 1 2	0 1 2	

APPENDIX 5

OLDER PERSONS' UNPLEASANT EVENTS SCHEDULE

	How often have these events occurred in your life in the past month?			How unpleasant is each event? *Rate whether or not event occurred in the past month.*		

	0 = Not at all
	1 = 1-6 times
	2 = 7 times
	    or more
				0 = Not unpleasant
				1 = Somewhat
				    unpleasant
				2 = Very unpleasant		

	Circle one number			Circle one number		Cross products
1. Arguments with spouse or living partner	0	1	2	0	1 2	
2. Being physically disabled	0	1	2	0	1 2	
3. Having a minor illness or injury	0	1	2	0	1 2	
4. Having my spouse (living partner, mate) dissatisfied with me	0	1	2	0	1 2	
5. Working on something I don't enjoy	0	1	2	0	1 2	
6. Having someone criticize or evaluate me	0	1	2	0	1 2	
7. Realizing that I can't do what I had thought I could	0	1	2	0	1 2	
8. Leaving a task uncompleted, procrastinating	0	1	2	0	1 2	
9. Working at something I don't care about	0	1	2	0	1 2	
10. Being near unpleasant people	0	1	2	0	1 2	
11. Having someone disagree with me	0	1	2	0	1 2	
12. Being insulted	0	1	2	0	1 2	
13. Having a project or assignment overdue	0	1	2	0	1 2	
14. Not having enough money	0	1	2	0	1 2	
15. Failing at something	0	1	2	0	1 2	
16. Being without privacy	0	1	2	0	1 2	
17. Working under pressure	0	1	2	0	1 2	
18. Performing poorly in sports	0	1	2	0	1 2	

	FREQUENCY	UNPLEASANTNESS	
	0 = Not at all 1 = 1-6 times 2 = 7 times or more	0 = Not unpleasant 1 = Somewhat unpleasant 2 = Very unpleasant	
	Circle one number	Circle one number	Cross product
19. Talking with an unpleasant person	0　1　2	0　1　2	
20. Realizing that someone I love and I are growing apart	0　1　2	0　1　2	
21. Doing something I don't want to do in order to please someone else	0　1　2	0　1　2	
22. Doing a job poorly	0　1　2	0　1　2	
23. Learning a friend or relative has just become ill or hospitalized	0　1　2	0　1　2	
24. Being told what to do	0　1　2	0　1　2	
25. Having a major unexpected expense (hospital bill, home repairs)	0　1　2	0　1　2	
26. Having family members or friends do something I disapprove of	0　1　2	0　1　2	
27. Learning that someone is angry with me or wants to hurt me	0　1　2	0　1　2	
28. Being nagged	0　1　2	0　1　2	
29. Being bothered with red tape, administrative hassles, paperwork	0　1　2	0　1　2	
30. Being away from someone I love	0　1　2	0　1　2	
31. Listening to people complain	0　1　2	0　1　2	
32. Having a relative or friend living in unsatisfactory surroundings	0　1　2	0　1　2	
33. Having to have a physical exam	0　1　2	0　1　2	
34. Being with other people when I don't choose to be	0　1　2	0　1　2	
35. Lying to someone	0　1　2	0　1　2	
36. Being asked something I could not or did not want to answer	0　1　2	0　1　2	
37. Doing something embarrassing in the presence of others	0　1　2	0　1　2	

	FREQUENCY 0 = Not at all 1 = 1-6 times 2 = 7 times or more			UNPLEASANTNESS 0 = Not unpleasant 1 = Somewhat unpleasant 2 = Very unpleasant		
	Circle one number			Circle one number		Cross product
38. Being clumsy	0	1	2	0	1	2
39. Having family members or friends do something that makes me ashamed	0	1	2	0	1	2
40. Not taking the planning time to be with people I care about	0	1	2	0	1	2
41. Having a friend with a health problem	0	1	2	0	1	2
42. Losing a friend	0	1	2	0	1	2
43. Listening to someone who doesn't stop talking	0	1	2	0	1	2
44. Living with a roommate who is in poor health	0	1	2	0	1	2
45. Being with sad people	0	1	2	0	1	2
46. Having people ignore what I said	0	1	2	0	1	2
47. Being physically uncomfortable	0	1	2	0	1	2
48. Having someone owe me money	0	1	2	0	1	2
49. Being misunderstood or misquoted	0	1	2	0	1	2
50. Being forced to do something	0	1	2	0	1	2
51. Having a sinus headache	0	1	2	0	1	2
52. Realizing I made a poor judgment	0	1	2	0	1	2
53. Having insomnia	0	1	2	0	1	2
54. Having loss of memory	0	1	2	0	1	2
55. Being limited to certain foods	0	1	2	0	1	2
56. Buying poor merchandise at high prices	0	1	2	0	1	2
57. Coping with insufficient funds	0	1	2	0	1	2
58. Hearing negative gossip	0	1	2	0	1	2
59. Being invaded of privacy	0	1	2	0	1	2
60. Having been taken advantage of	0	1	2	0	1	2

	FREQUENCY	UNPLEASANTNESS
	0 = Not at all **1 = 1-6 times** **2 = 7 times** **or more**	**0 = Not unpleasant** **1 = Somewhat** **unpleasant** **2 = Very unpleasant**

	Circle one number	Circle one number	Cross product
61. Inattentiveness during a conversation	0 1 2	0 1 2	
62. Seeing people enjoy depression	0 1 2	0 1 2	
63. Having to work when tired	0 1 2	0 1 2	
64. Being awakened when I am trying to sleep	0 1 2	0 1 2	

APPENDIX 6

DAILY MOOD RATING FORM

1. Please rate your mood for this day (i.e., how good or bad you felt) using the 9-point scale shown below. If you felt good put a high number on the chart below. If you felt "so-so" mark 5, and if you felt low or depressed mark a number lower than 5.

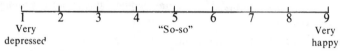

1	2	3	4	5	6	7	8	9
Very depressed				"So-so"				Very happy

2. On the two lines next to your mood rating for each day, please briefly give two major reasons why you think you felt that way. Try to be as specific as possible.

Date	Mood Score	Why I think I felt this way
		1.
		2.
		1.
		2.
		1.
		2.
		1.
		2.
		1.
		2.
		1.
		2.
		1.
		2.
		1.
		2.
		1.
		2.
		1.
		2.

APPENDIX 7

DAILY PLEASANT ACTIVITIES TRACKING SHEET

Name _____

Note: Check box only if activity both occurred and was considered at least a little pleasant by you.

Activity	Date & Day of Week						
1.							
2.							
3.							
4.							
5.							
6.							
7.							
8.							
9.							
10.							
11.							
12.							
13.							
14.							
15.							
16.							
17.							
18.							
19.							
20.							
21.							
22.							
23.							
24.							
25.							
26.							
28.							
28.							
29.							
30.							
31.							
32.							
33.							
34.							
35.							
36.							
37.							
38.							
39.							
40.							

APPENDIX 8

DAILY UNPLEASANT ACTIVITIES TRACKING SHEET

Name _____

Note: Check box only if activity both occurred and was considered at least a little unpleasant by you.

Activity	Date & Day of Week						
1.							
2.							
3.							
4.							
5.							
6.							
7.							
8.							
9.							
10.							
11.							
12.							
13.							
14.							
15.							
16.							
17.							
18.							
19.							
20.							
21.							
22.							
23.							
24.							
25.							
26.							
28.							
28.							
29.							
30.							
31.							
32.							
33.							
34.							
35.							
36.							
37.							
38.							
39.							
40.							

APPENDIX 9

MEANS AND STANDARD DEVIATIONS
OF THE PLEASANT AND UNPLEASANT EVENTS SCALES FOR OLDER PERSONS*

	Frequency Score	Feeling Score (Pleasantness or Unpleasantness)	Cross Product (Frequency times Feeling)
Pleasant Events Scale (N = 66)			
Mean	1.372	1.662	2.476
Standard Deviation	0.277	0.238	0.680
Unpleasant Events Scale (N = 64)			
Mean	0.870	1.806	1.118
Standard Deviation	0.458	0.496	0.671

*The modification of scales developed by Lewinsohn, Munoz, Youngren, & Zeiss (1978). Data provided through the courtesy of Bonnie Hedlund and Michael Gilewski, unpublished manuscript, University of Southern California, 1981.

APPENDIX 10

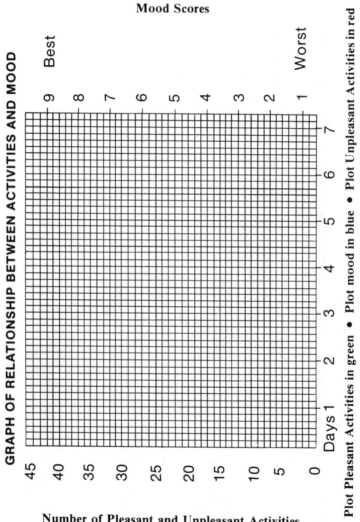

GRAPH OF RELATIONSHIP BETWEEN ACTIVITIES AND MOOD

Mood Scores

Best 9 8 7 6 5 4 3 2 1 Worst

Days 1 2 3 4 5 6 7

45 40 35 30 25 20 15 10 5 0

Number of Pleasant and Unpleasant Activities

Plot Pleasant Activities in green ● Plot mood in blue ● Plot Unpleasant Activities in red

Date: From _____ to _____

APPENDIX 11

LEARNING HOW TO GET COMPLETELY RELAXED

I. Rules for Progressive Relaxation Training

This section presents all the rules you need to know and follow when practicing progressive relaxation. The techniques you are going to learn about are based on the work of physiologist Dr. Edmund Jacobsen. His procedures have come to be known as Progressive Relaxation Training. They are readily adapted to a self-administered program and are relatively easy to learn.

It is important to stress that progressive relaxation is a skill. In this respect progressive relaxation is very different from programs such as hypnosis. During hypnosis, a trained person makes strong suggestions in order to induce a state of relaxation. In progressive relaxation you teach yourself how to relax and you are the one who controls how you feel. You don't put yourself in a "trance" or lose control over your feelings. Instead you learn how to gain control over tension in your muscles in order to enjoy the more comfortable feelings of relaxation.

Because progressive relaxation is a skill, it can only be learned if you take the time to practice. In this respect your relaxation training program is just like sewing, cooking, or any other skill that must be learned through practice. Don't worry if your progress seems slow. As long as you work at the procedures and practice conscientiously, you will experience an enjoyable state of relaxation by the end of your program.

In progressive relaxation training you learn how to identify the feeling of muscular relaxation by alternately tensing and relaxing different muscle groups in your body. The best way to illustrate what this means is to have you practice a demonstration trial right now. Take your dominant hand (if you're right-handed use your right hand, if left-handed use your left hand) and make a loose fist without applying any pressure. Continue to read these instructions and when you come across the word "now" in big capital letters you should tighten your fist and notice the tension you produce. You'll probably feel tension in your knuckles, in your fingers, and in other parts of your hand. You may also feel tension spreading into the lower part of your arm. When you make the fist, hold it for about five to seven seconds. Then, when you see the word "relax" in capital letters, throw away the tension by quickly opening your hand and relaxing the muscles.

Once more, let's review the sequence. When you see the word "now", you will tense your fist and locate where the points of tension are for you. After five to seven seconds you will quickly release that tension and experience an increase in relaxation. Get ready by making yourself comfortable. Have your arms resting on the arm of the chair you are in and *NOW* tighten your fist and hold it. Do you feel tension in your fingers? In your knuckles? Does the tension spread to your wrist and forearm? Briefly study the tension in your hand and now *RELAX* your fist. Rest your hand comfortably on the chair or in your lap and experience the tension leaving your lower arm. You shouldn't expect your hand to feel totally relaxed. That takes practice. But you should experience some of the tension that you purposefully put into your muscles leaving the tense areas. It doesn't matter if the effects you feel are large or small and it doesn't matter if your hand still feels a little tense. The purpose of this demonstration was just to help you learn the basic procedural components of relaxation training. *By alternatively tensing and relaxing your muscles you will learn how to identify tension and bring about a state of relaxation.*

A. Review of Muscle Groups

At this point it would help to review for you the different muscle groups that you will practice during your relaxation sessions. As you read these instructions remember that you are not actually practicing relaxation training now. You are simply learning the muscle groups that will be involved during your practice sessions later on. Spend as much time as you need on this section in order to become familiar with this list. You will notice that there are 15 muscles which have been grouped into four Major Muscle Groups. As you read down the list try to see which methods for creating tension are best suited for your individual muscles. To do this you should briefly create a little tension in each of the muscle groups as you follow along with the list. By checking this now, you'll know how to best create tension during your actual practice sessions. Use the next page for recording which method of tensing is best suited for each of your muscle groups. This page can then be placed in your notebook and kept for future reference.

Major Muscle Group 1: The Hands and Arms

Dominant Hand and Forearm. This is the muscle group you just tensed by making a fist and holding it tight.
Dominant Biceps: To tense this group you should keep your arm flat on the chair while pushing down with your elbow. It's as if you are trying to push your elbow into the arm of the chair. Try this now. If this method does not create tension in your biceps, you can bend your arm at the elbow bringing your hand towards your

shoulder. Then apply what is called a "counterforce." To do this, try to touch your shoulder with your hand while at the same time opposing this movement. This should make your hand feel as if it is frozen in the air as you try to move it up towards your shoulder while at the same time wanting it to fall back down.

Nondominant Hand and Forearm. Just like before, make a fist, but this time use your nondominant hand.

Nondominant Biceps. Follow the same procedure described for the dominant biceps.

Major Muscle Group 2: The Head, Face, and Throat

The muscles in this group are very important since many people experience their greatest amounts of tension in the facial muscles.

Forehead. To tense the muscles in your forehead try lifting your eyebrows high as if you want to touch the top of your head. An alternative method is to frown or "knit your brows."

Upper Cheeks and Nose. To tense the muscles in this area, squint your eyes and wrinkle your nose. Don't be afraid of making funny faces when you're practicing.

Lower Cheeks and Jaws. These muscles can be tensed by biting or clenching your teeth together hard and pulling back the corners of your mouth.

Lips and Tongue. Press your tongue against the top of your mouth and at the same time pucker or press your lips together.

Neck and Throat. Tension in your neck and throat is achieved by again using a counterforce. Pull your chin down as if you are trying to touch your chest. Now apply a counterpressure as if you are trying to stop your chin from touching your chest. If this method doesn't work, a good alternative is to press your head back against your chair. Of course, in order to do this you need to be sitting in a chair with a tall back. Alternatively, you can prop yourself up against a bed headboard.

Major Muscle Group 3: The Chest and Stomach

These muscles are very important. When the actual practice sessions start, you will notice that controlled breathing is an extremely useful way to increase the general level of relaxation throughout your body.

Chest. To tense the muscles in your chest, take a deep breath and hold it. Then exhale slowly and notice the immediate sensations of relaxation that spread across your muscles.

Shoulders and Upper Back. Tense these muscles by pulling your shoulders up. Pretend they are being held there by strings attached to the ceiling. Simultaneously arch your shoulders back and try to touch your shoulder blades together.

Abdominal or Stomach Area. These muscles are most easily tensed by simply making your stomach hard as if you're going to be hit in the stomach. If you have difficulty doing this, you can try pulling your stomach in and holding it tight, or, alternatively, pushing your stomach out.

Major Muscle Group 4: The Legs and Feet

The muscles in your legs and feet constitute the last Major Muscle Group for you to learn. Once you have learned to relax all of your muscles you will be able to experience soothing relaxation throughout your arms, face, chest, abdomen, and all the way down to your feet.

Thighs and Buttocks. Tense the muscles in these areas by pressing your heels into the ground and tightening the muscles in your buttocks. An alternative counterforce method involves pressing your knees towards each other while at the same time applying pressure in your muscles to keep them apart. If neither of these methods produce noticeable tension in your thighs and buttocks, you can try lifting your legs straight out in front of you and holding them there.

Calves. Point your toes up towards your head. Alternatively, you can point your toes down, away from your head.

Feet. These muscles can tense up quickly. Rather than hold the tension in these muscles for 5 to 7 seconds, you should use a 3 to 5 second period. In order to tense these muscles, point your toes slightly down, turn your feet in, and curl your toes.

B. Possible Problems

Distractions. It is impossible to attain a satisfactory level of relaxation if there are distractions in your external environment. For this reason, it is extremely important that you find a quiet room that affords you complete privacy. Also be sure that you have a stuffed chair or a place to lie down that is sufficiently comfortable.

It's also a good idea to avoid all unnecessary movement while you are relaxing. Use your muscles as little as possible. Behaviors such as laughing, talking, sneezing, coughing, and general body movements (fidgeting) are to be avoided during your practice sessions. It will probably be helpful if you take measures to purposefully avoid distracting behaviors. Finding yourself a private room and keeping external distractions such as outside noises to a minimum should help. If you have a cold you may need to postpone one of your sessions because of constant sneezing. If you have a problem with smoker's cough, it may help to inhale less deeply during your practice sessions. Use your own judgment when arranging your environment so that distracting factors are kept to a minimum.

Intrusive Thoughts. Intrusive thoughts which interefere with relaxation can be a problem. Most commonly these difficulties center around anxiety-producing thoughts or thoughts which concern feelings of sexual arousal. If you find that unpleasant or arousing thoughts preoccupy your thinking while you relax, do not become concerned. This type of difficulty is common, and after general practice sessions its distracting influence will lessen on its own.

If you would like to actively counteract disruptive thoughts, you can purposefully call to mind pleasant imagery. For example, if you couldn't stop thinking about a particular incident that made you tense, you could concentrate your mind on a different scene that helped you relax. Perhaps you could imagine yourself sitting under a tree on a beautiful spring day. Add details to this pleasant scene to make it more real for you. If scenes with green grass and clear blue skies are not relaxing, make up a scene on your own that helps to counteract distracting thoughts.

Unpleasant Feelings. Some of you may feel that you are losing control as you "float" into a state of relaxation. If you experience this feeling as a problem, you should probably approach the program at a slower pace. This will help you appreciate that you are actually producing all of your own sensations. Through practice you will see that you are the real director of what you feel and you can control how relaxed you want to be.

It is also possible that some of you may experience relaxation in your exterior muscles but still feel tense inside. This is not unusual, and should not cause concern. With practice, feelings of relaxation will usually extend themselves throughout your entire body.

A number of miscellaneous reactions that may occur should also be mentioned. At times you may experience small muscle spasms or jerks while relaxing your muscles. You may also experience tingling or floating sensations. If these feelings are in your head they can even be dizzying at times. If it is any comfort to you, these reactions are not unusual. In fact, they are signals that you are actually succeding at relaxing your muscle groups. With practice these reactions will either diminish or become familiar to you. By the end of your sessions they will not be problems. Some sensations such as the experience of "floating" can even become enjoyable when associated with deep relaxation.

Additional Problems. Naturally it is important that you avoid falling asleep during your sessions. If you find yourself dozing off you can clearly feel confident that your efforts to relax are successful. Unfortunately, once you are asleep you can no longer practice.

Effectively developing your skills does require that you work at the procedures, so try to stay awake.

If you experience a muscle cramp while practicing, all you need to do is reduce the time interval that you use for tensing the muscles. Alternatively, you can apply less force when making your muscles tight.

It is possible that certain areas of your body may still feel tense when the program outlined in this manual is completed. If this happens, you may want to add some additional muscles on your own. For example, let's say you have finished the program but still experience tension in your lower back. In this case you would want to try out different positions for tensing these muscles. Once you have successfully identified how to tense the muscles in your back you would follow the procedures of alternative tension and relaxation that you have already learned.

C. Using the Cassette Tape Recorder

If you have a cassette tape recorder, your therapist will tape the instructions for deep muscle relaxation. It is important that you use this properly in order to have success with the program. Recent evidence suggests that recorded instructions may be less effective than instructions given by a live therapist. It is believed that this may be due to the tape progressing from one muscle group to the next without stopping to see how you're doing. For example, a tape might tell you to tense your biceps and then relax them. Perhaps you should really practice this five times in order to fully relax, but the taped instructions repeat the message only twice. It then goes right along and tells you to tense and relax your forehead. Because the tape does not take your progress into account, you should *not* use the tape during your training sessions.

The proper way to use the tape is to have it serve as a model. In other words, by listening to the tape you can learn what kinds of instructions to give yourself during your actual practice sessions. Listening to the tape will help you know how to pace your instructions and how to talk to yourself about relaxing and tensing. Although the tape can help demonstrate the instructions you will use, be sure to remember that you are your own instructor. *During your practice sessions, you should proceed from one muscle group to the next on your own—without listening to the tape—and at your own pace.*

D. Learning the Instructions

In order to become familiar with the instructions used during relaxation practice sessions, you should now listen to the tape. As you listen to the instructions, do not actually tense your muscles. Instead, concentrate on learning how to instruct yourself in tension and relaxation. Notice how, on the tape, the voice changes its tone from one part to the next. When the instructios are telling you to tense a muscle the voice is crisp and sharp. When you are being told to relax, the voice is calm and soothing. During your practice sessions you will want to also vary your expressions. You'll want the "feeling" of your instructions to complement the opposing moods of tension and relaxation.

Go ahead now and listen to the tape. If you don't have a cassette recorder and are unable to borrow a friend's, you can study the set of instructions accompanying your program. These instructions are identical to those on the record. Some of you with a recorder may even want to read along as you listen to your tape. After you have become familiar with the type of instructions used in progressive relaxation training, you should return to this handout and study the next section.

E. An Example

To further help you learn how to self-administer relaxation instructions, you should study the following example. This example specifically mentions the forehead, but you can substitute any muscle group and still use similar expressions. Alternate expressions from the above lists can also be used.

While you are reading these instructions, you don't want to actually tense and relax your muscles. You will not begin progressive relaxation training until the next chapter. Right now you are simply learning the kinds of instructions you'll be using. Go ahead, then, and study the example given below while repeating the instructions to yourself.

> Relax your entire body to the best of your ability. Settle back, and as you are relaxing, wrinkle up your forehead. *NOW...* keep your forehead wrinkled ... tighter ... experience the tightness take over your muscles and now ... *RELAX* ... throw away the tightness in your muscles and do the opposite of tension ... relax ... let go of all the tension and spread the feelings of relaxation all over ... experience the contrast between tension and relaxation ... once again, *NOW* wrinkle your forehead ... that's right, put tension back into your muscles and again study this tension ... hold the tension in your muscles and now *RELAX* again and enjoy the contrast ... spread the relaxation over your face further ... continue this process ... relax ... relax.

Read the above example again. Practice creating a feeling of tension in your own mind as you repeat to yourself the instructional portions that tell you to tense the muscles. Then try to experience a lazy calm feeling of restfulness as you read the sections that instruct you to relax. You should probably practice these instructions several times. Try varying the expressions in order to become more familiar with different phrases. You can also make up new phrases of your own if you feel more comfortable using them.

NOTE: You want to practice saying these instructions to yourself *SILENTLY.* Saying them out loud would interfere with relaxation during your actual practice sessions.

F. Review

These are the things you should have done while reading this section. Check off the ones you have done:

a. _____ Learned what the basic procedures of progressive relaxation training are and practiced the single demonstration with your hand.

b. _____ Learned the different muscle groups you will be practicing and recorded which methods you will be using when tensing each group.

c. _____ Acquired some idea of the possible problems you may have while practicing so you will not be overconcerned if you run into difficulties.

You now should have all the information you need to begin relaxation practicing. Since you have covered a lot this session, it is best to wait until tomorrow to actually begin practice sessions.

You should plan your practice sessions now, however. Following these instructions you will find a Log Sheet to use to schedule *in advance* your practice sessions. Try to schedule two sessions a day. You should not, however, practice relaxation at bedtime yet. *You need to get good at relaxing first.* When you can relax with ease, the program will guide you in how to use this skill for getting to sleep. This will take about a week if you practice twice a day.

II. Practicing Relaxation

This section presents in detail the structure of the program you should follow to learn progressive relaxation. It is important that you work carefully. Do not move on to a new part of the training program before you have successfully completed an earlier part.

Be certain that your practice sessions are held in a quiet room that allows you complete privacy and total comfort. You should go ahead now and find yourself that comfortable place we've talked about. A good padded chair with a high back is preferable, but a place where you can comfortably lie down is also adequate. Make sure the lighting and noise levels are relaxing. Set everything up the way you want it and make yourself comfortable before you continue reading these instructions.

A. Practicing the First Major Group

Now that you've found a comfortable place, here's what you'll be doing. The following rules apply to all of the muscle groups you'll be practicing.

When you first practice a particular muscle group such as your hand, you should tense the muscles for a period of 5-7 seconds. The only exceptions to this rule are your feet and other muscle groups that may have a tendency to cramp. When practicing the feet and any other groups which tend to cramp, you should decrease the tension period to 3-5 seconds.

Naturally, you don't want to tense your muscles so hard that it hurts. You simply want to use sufficient pressure to allow you to identify points of muscle tension.

After you have tensed your muscles for the 5-7 second tension period, you should actively throw away the tension by quickly releasing your hold on the muscles. Then, for a period of 15 to 20 seconds, spend your time consciously extending the feelings of relaxation through your muscles. During this relaxation period, concentrate on the contrast between tension and relaxation. Remember that even when you feel relaxed some muscle fibers may still be contracted. Relaxing is an active process of undoing tension, and you want to extend the activity of relaxing as far as possible.

You should practice tensing and relaxing each of the muscle groups at least twice before proceeding to a new group. You'll probably find that the second time you tense your muscles, the particular points of tension become more apparent. Through practice, you will get better at identifying these sources of tension; you will also get better at relaxing the tension away.

If, after practicing a particular muscle group twice, you feel a deep sense of relaxation without any residual tension, you should proceed to the next muscle group on your list. If, however, you are able to still feel tension in your muscles, you should continue to practice the same muscle group. If these muscles continue to feel tense after five practice trials, you should stop and go on to the next group.

Now let's review these rules again. You should practice each group twice, and move on to the next group whenever your muscles feel relaxed. If your muscles maintain a perceptible degree of tension, you should practice as many as five times in a single session before moving on to the next group.

Don't be concerned or worried about failures, even if you feel tension in several muscle groups after practicing them five times each. Learning progressive relaxation skills takes time and hard work. Some of you will need to spend as many as six sessions or more. A reasonable goal to be setting for this first session is to simply acquire the idea or swing of things. Expecting to be instantly relaxed in a single session is unrealistic.

The rules just reviewed will be followed for each of the muscle groups listed in the previous chapter. For the time being, however, you should practice only the muscles in the First Major Group. This includes your dominant and nondominant hands, forearms, and biceps. Put your manual down now and begin to practice each muscle in the First Major Group following the rules that were just outlined. Practice each group at least twice, but no more than five times. When you're done with this first set of muscles, return to the instructions below.

B. Practicing the Remaining Major Groups

Good. You have now had an actual practice session with all of the muscles in the First Major Group. Before going straight on to the forehead and other muscles in the Second Major Group, you should practice an additional and useful exercise. Whenever you finish all of the muscles in a particular major group, you should take a break for about 40 to 60 seconds. Now, taking a break doesn't mean that you get up and stop practicing. Instead, a break means that you take some time to really relax all of the muscles you previously practiced before going right on to the next muscle group. You should spend this time extending your feelings of relaxation further and further so you experience even greater levels of comfort. To do this you should go over in your mind each of the muscle groups and say to yourself the relaxing expressions you have already learned. Also, be sure to use to your advantage the relaxing effects of exhaling slowly. Each time you exhale think to yourself the word "relax" or the word "calm." Exhaling slowly and evenly seems to carry people into deeper levels of relaxation. It's a good feeling. With practice you can learn to take full advantage of it.

In order to have read this section, you had to disrupt the relaxation in your arms and biceps. Fortunately, you won't have to do that again, since you now know the entire sequence of rules. First, you practice each muscle group at least twice. (If you feel tension, you can practice the same group up to five times in a single session.) When you have finished all the muscles in a major group, you take a break and extend your relaxation to deeper and deeper levels. After taking this break and reviewing your completed muscles, you can go on to the muscles in the next major group, practicing them in the same way. Follow this procedure until you have finished all of the muscles in all of the major groups, or until you have spent about forty minutes. When you are ready to stop for the day, be sure to first come back to the manual and read the next short section.

C. Relaxation Training Procedures

A standard set of instructions for tensing and relaxing the major muscle groups discussed follows. You may want to practice now, using these instructions, before moving on to the rest of this handout.

Relaxation of Arms (Time: 4-5 minutes)

Settle back as comfortably as you can. Let yourself relax to the best of your ability ... Now, as you relax like that, clench your right fist, just clench your fist tighter and tighter, and study the tension as you do so. Keep it clenched and feel the tension in your right fist, hand, forearm ... Now relax. Let the fingers of your right hand become loose, and observe the contrast in your feelings ... Now let yourself go and try to become more relaxed all over ... Once more, clench your right fist really tight ... hold it and notice the tension again ... Now let go, relax; your fingers straighten out, and you notice the difference once more ... Now repeat that with your left fist. Clench your left fist while the rest of your body relaxes; clench that fist tighter and feel the tension ... and now relax. Again enjoy the contrast ... Repeat that once more, clench the left fist, tight and tense ... Now do the opposite of tension—relax and feel the difference. Continue relaxing like that for awhile ... Clench both fists tighter and tighter, both fists tense, forearms tense, study the sensations ... and relax; straighten out your fingers and feel that relaxation. Continue relaxing your hands and forearms more and more ... Now bend your elbows and tense your biceps, tense them harder and study the tension feelings ... all right, straighten out your arms, let them relax and feel that difference again. Let the relaxation develop ... Once more, tense your biceps; hold the tension and observe it carefully ... Straighten the arms and relax; relax to the best of your ability ... Each time, pay close attention to your feelings when you tense up and when you relax. Now straighten your arms, straighten them so that you feel most tension in the triceps muscles along the back of your arms. Stretch your arms and feel that tension ... And now relax. Get your arms back into a comfortable position. Let the relaxation proceed on its own. The arms should feel comfortably heavy as you allow them to relax ... Straighten the arms once more so that you feel the tension in the triceps muscles; straighten them. Feel that tension ... and relax. Get the arms comfortable and let them relax further and further. Continue relaxing your arms ever further. Even when your arms seem fully relaxed, try to go even further; try to achieve deeper and deeper levels of relaxation.

Relaxation of Facial Area with Neck, Shoulders, and Upper Back (Time: 4-5 minutes)

Relax your entire body to the best of your ability. Feel that comfortable heaviness. Let all your muscles go loose and heavy. Just settle back quietly and comfortably. Wrinkle up your forehead now; wrinkle it tighter ... And now stop wrinkling your forehead; relax and smooth it out. Picture the entire forehead and scalp becoming smoother as the relaxation increases ... Now frown and crease your brows and study the tension ... Let go of the tension again. Smooth out the forehead once more ... Now, close your eyes tighter and tighter ... feel the tension ... and relax yor eyes. Keep your eyes closed, gently, comfortably, and notice the relaxation ... Now clench your jaws, bite your teeth together; study the tension throughout the jaws ... Relax your jaws now. Let your lips part slightly ... Appreciate the relaxation ... Now press your tongue hard against the roof of your mouth. Look for the tension ... All right, let your tongue return to a comfortable and relaxed position ... Now purse your lips, press your lips together tighter and tighter ... Relax the lips. Note that contrast between tension and relaxation. Feel the relaxation all over your face, all over your forehead and scalp, eyes, jaws, lips, tongue and your neck muscles. Press your head back as far as it can go and feel the tension in the neck; roll it to the right and feel the tension shift; now roll it to the left. Straighten your head and bring it forward, press your chin against your chest. Let your head return to a comfortable position, and study the relaxation. Let the relaxation develop ... Shrug your shoulders, right up. Hold the tension ... Drop your shoulders and feel the relaxation. Neck and shoulders relaxed ... Shrug your shoulders again and move them around. Bring your shoulders up and forward and back. Feel the tension in your shoulders and in your upper back ... Drop your shoulders once more and relax. Let the relaxation spread deep into the shoulders, right into your back muscles; relax your neck and throat, and your jaws and other facial areas as the pure relaxation takes over and grows deeper ... deeper ... ever deeper.

Relaxation of Chest, Stomach, and Lower Back (Time: 4-5 minutes)

Relax your entire body to the best of your ability. Feel that comfortable heaviness that accompanies relaxation. Breathe easily and freely in and out. Notice how the relaxation increases as you exhale ... as you breathe out just feel that relaxation ... Now breathe right in and fill your lungs; inhale deeply and hold your breath. Study the tension ... Now exhale, let the walls of your chest grow loose and push the air out automatically. Continue relaxing and breathe freely and gently. Feel the relaxation and enjoy it ...

With the rest of your body as relaxed as possible, fill your lungs again. Breathe in deeply and hold it again. That's fine, breathe out and appreciate the relief. Just breathe normally. Continue relaxing your chest and let the relaxation spread to your back, shoulders, neck and arms. Merely let go ... and enjoy the relaxation. Now let's pay attention to your abdominal muscles, your stomach area. Tighten your stomach muscles, make your abdomen hard. Notice the tension ... and relax. Let the muscles loosen and notice the contrast ... Once more, press and tighten your stomach muscles. Hold the tension and study it ... And relax. Notice the general well-being that comes with relaxing your stomach ... Now draw your stomach in, pull the muscles right in and feel the tension this way ... Now relax again. Let your stomach out. Continue breathing normally and easily and feel the gentle massaging action all over your chest and stomach ... Now pull your stomach in again and hold the tension ... Now push out and tense like that; hold the tension ... once more pull in and feel the tension ... now relax your stomach fully. Let the tension dissolve as the relaxation grows deeper. Each time you breathe out, notice the rhythmic relaxation both in your lungs and in your stomach. Notice thereby how your chest and your stomach relax more and more ... Try and let go of all contractions anywhere in your body ... Now direct your attention to your lower back. Arch up your back, make your lower back quite hollow, and feel the tension along your spine ... and settle down comfortably again relaxing the lower back ... Just arch your back up and feel the tensions as you do so. Try to keep the rest of the body as relaxed as possible. Try to localize the tension throughout your lower back area ... Relax once more, relaxing further and further. Relax your lower back, relax your upper back, spread the relaxation to your stomach, chest, shoulders, arms and facial area. These parts relaxing further and further and further and ever deeper.

Relaxation of Hips, Thighs, and Calves, Followed by Complete Body Relaxation (Time: 4-5 minutes)

Let go of all tensions and relax ... Now flex your buttocks and thighs. Flex your thighs by pressing down your heels as hard as you can ... Relax and note difference. Straighten your knees and flex your thigh muscles again. Hold the tension ... Relax your hips and thighs. Allow the relaxation to proceed on its own ... Press your feet and toes downwards, away from your face, so that your calf muscles become tense. Study that tension ... Relax your feet and calves ... This time, bend your feet towards your face so that you feel tension along your shins. Bring your toes right up ... Relax again. Keep relaxing for a while ... Now let yourself relax further all over. Relax your feet, ankles, calves, and shins; knees, thighs, buttocks, and hips. Feel the heaviness of your lower body as you relax still further ... Now spread the relaxation to your stomach, waist, lower back. Let go more and more deeply. Make sure that no tension has crept into your throat; relax your neck and your jaws and all your facial muscles. Keep relaxing your whole body like that for a while. Let yourself relax.

Now you can become twice as relaxed as you are merely by taking in a really deep breath and slowly exhaling. With your eyes closed so that you become less aware of objects and movements around you and thus prevent any surface tension from developing, breathe in deeply and feel yourself becoming heavier. Take in a long, deep breath, and let it out very slowly ... Feel how heavy and relaxed you have become.

In a state of perfect relaxation, you should feel unwilling to move a single muscle in your body. Think about the effort that would be required to raise your right arm. As you think about raising your right arm, see if you can notice any tensions that might have crept into your shoulder and your arm ... Now you decide not to lift the arm, but to continue relaxing. Observe the relief and the disappearance of the tension...

Just carry on relaxing like that. When you wish to get up, count backwards from four to one. You should then feel fine and refreshed; wideawake and calm.

D. Rating Your Relaxation

You have now finished your first practice session of Relaxation. On your Log Sheet there is a Relaxation Rating scale with numbers from 1 to 10, where 1 indicates the least relaxed you have ever been and 10 is the most relaxed you have ever been. Rate the extent of your relaxation by circling the one number that most appropriately describes the extent of your relaxation. You should rate your relaxation in this manner immediately following each practice session of relaxation.

E. Practice Sessions 2 Through 4, and Maybe Even 6!

You have now had a single regularly scheduled session for relaxation training. If your progress has been rapid you may have experienced little difficulty working through all of the muscle groups on your list. But it's more likely that you have simply succeeded in appreciating the difference between tension and relaxation. While some of your muscle groups were easily relaxed, you probably had trouble completely relaxing all of them. It is also possible that some of you are moving along even more slowly. Perhaps you have been able to notice only very subtle differences between tension and relaxation.

Depending on your progress it may be possible for you to start making predictions about the time you'll need to successfully achieve deep levels of progressive relaxation. If you are one of those "quick" individuals, you may only need to spend one or two more sessions on this part of your program. If you are one of the more "typical" people, you can plan on spending two to four additional sessions. Finally, if you are a "slow" relaxer (which is not at all uncommon), you'll probably want to spend five to six more sessions. Regardless of the number of sessions it takes to learn progressive relaxation, all of you can achieve the same level of success in the end.

What you practice today depends, of course, on the progress you've made in earlier sessions. Continue to employ the same rules you've been using until you are able to easily relax each of the various muscle groups in two trials. Use your regularly scheduled sessions to practice all the groups in their regular order. Then, use your practice sessions to work on especially difficult muscle groups. If you run into difficulties it would be a good idea to go back and read the list of possible problems that was presented in the previous chapter. Check and be sure you produce noticeable levels of tension during the tensing phases of your exercises. Check to see that you are not letting your mind wander to negative or anxious thoughts. If you have this problem, remember to substitute your negative thoughts with positive and pleasant imagery. Also, take advantage of the relaxing effects associated with slow, even breathing.

Go ahead now and try at least two sessions of relaxation. You should spend as many regular sessions as necessary to learn how to successfully relax all of the muscle groups on your list. You may accomplish this goal at the end of your second training session ... but it may not be until your fourth or even your sixth.

III. Evaluating Your Progress

Have you done at least two relaxation sessions?

Yes _____ *Go on to the next questions.*

No _____ Keep practicing until you have done two sessions.

Have you been able to achieve relaxation which you rated as 7 or better on at least one of the two sessions?

Yes _____ Return to the module you were working on. You are now ready to use your relaxation skills.

No _____ You probably need more practice. Try it four more times. If you are still having trouble, bring it up at your next treatment session.

METHODS USED TO TENSE THE MUSCLE GROUPS

Muscle Group	Method of Tensing
Dominant hand and forearm	
Dominant biceps	
Nondominant hand and forearm	
Nondominant biceps	
Forehead	
Upper cheeks and nose	
Lower cheeks and jaws	
Lips and tongue	
Neck and throat	
Chest	
Shoulders and upper back	
Abdominal or stomach area	
Thighs and buttocks	
Calves	
Feet	

RELAXATION LOG SHEET

Whenever you practice relaxation, record it below. Under
"Comment," indicate how long the session was and what you
worked on. Then circle the appropriate number under "Relaxation
Rating" to indicate the extent of your relaxation at the end of that
session (1 indicates that you were not relaxed at all; 10 indicates that
you were relaxed as you have ever been).

Session	Day/Date	Time	Comments	Relaxation Rating
1				1 2 3 4 5 6 7 8 9 10
2				1 2 3 4 5 6 7 8 9 10
3				1 2 3 4 5 6 7 8 9 10
4				1 2 3 4 5 6 7 8 9 10
5				1 2 3 4 5 6 7 8 9 10
6				1 2 3 4 5 6 7 8 9 10
7				1 2 3 4 5 6 7 8 9 10
8				1 2 3 4 5 6 7 8 9 10
9				1 2 3 4 5 6 7 8 9 10
10				1 2 3 4 5 6 7 8 9 10
11				1 2 3 4 5 6 7 8 9 10
12				1 2 3 4 5 6 7 8 9 10
13				1 2 3 4 5 6 7 8 9 10
14				1 2 3 4 5 6 7 8 9 10
15				1 2 3 4 5 6 7 8 9 10
16				1 2 3 4 5 6 7 8 9 10
17				1 2 3 4 5 6 7 8 9 10
18				1 2 3 4 5 6 7 8 9 10
19				1 2 3 4 5 6 7 8 9 10
20				1 2 3 4 5 6 7 8 9 10
21				1 2 3 4 5 6 7 8 9 10
22				1 2 3 4 5 6 7 8 9 10
23				1 2 3 4 5 6 7 8 9 10
24				1 2 3 4 5 6 7 8 9 10

Session	Day/Date	Time	Comments	Relaxation Rating
25				1 2 3 4 5 6 7 8 9 10
26				1 2 3 4 5 6 7 8 9 10
27				1 2 3 4 5 6 7 8 9 10
28				1 2 3 4 5 6 7 8 9 10
29				1 2 3 4 5 6 7 8 9 10
30				1 2 3 4 5 6 7 8 9 10
31				1 2 3 4 5 6 7 8 9 10
32				1 2 3 4 5 6 7 8 9 10
33				1 2 3 4 5 6 7 8 9 10
34				1 2 3 4 5 6 7 8 9 10
35				1 2 3 4 5 6 7 8 9 10
36				1 2 3 4 5 6 7 8 9 10
37				1 2 3 4 5 6 7 8 9 10
38				1 2 3 4 5 6 7 8 9 10
39				1 2 3 4 5 6 7 8 9 10
40				1 2 3 4 5 6 7 8 9 10
41				1 2 3 4 5 6 7 8 9 10
42				1 2 3 4 5 6 7 8 9 10
43				1 2 3 4 5 6 7 8 9 10
44				1 2 3 4 5 6 7 8 9 10
45				1 2 3 4 5 6 7 8 9 10
46				1 2 3 4 5 6 7 8 9 10
47				1 2 3 4 5 6 7 8 9 10
48				1 2 3 4 5 6 7 8 9 10
49				1 2 3 4 5 6 7 8 9 10
50				1 2 3 4 5 6 7 8 9 10

APPENDIX 12

HOW TO RELAX IN REAL LIFE SITUATIONS

Covert and Overt Techniques to be Learned

These materials will teach you how to relax in situations that now cause you anxiety or discomfort. This program involves covert and real life practice of relaxation in problem situations. "Covert" means to practice in your imagination, and by practicing relaxation responses in your imagination and then later in real life situations, you will become more and more able to remain comfortable in situations that now make you tense or anxious.

Practicing Relaxation Responses Covertly

The first step in covert practice of relaxation responses is to PICK A TYPE OF SITUATION ON WHICH YOU WANT TO WORK. *This involves writing a brief description of a type of situation which makes you uncomfortable on your Covert Rehearsal Practice Record. The Covert Rehearsal Practice Record is on the next page.*

Write your description under the column headed "Type of Situation." The situation you pick could be quite general or fairly specific. For example, if you find that you are often uncomfortable when going to the doctor's office, list "going to the doctor's office." As another example, if going into restaurants makes you uncomfortable, list "eating in a restaurant." The type of situation you choose should be one that is important to you, however. By picking the type of situation you want to work on, you make it more likely that these exercises will help with uncomfortable situations that are important to you.

The second step in the covert rehearsal of relaxation responses is to CHOOSE A SPECIFIC INSTANCE OF THE TYPE OF SITUATION YOU WANT TO WORK ON. *This involves writing an example of the type of situation you want to work on under the column headed "Specific Instance" on your Covert Rehearsal Practice Record.* For example, if the type of situation you list is "being in a noisy store," your specific instance might be "being at X department store on a holiday sale day." Or, if the type of situation you list is "being alone in a strange place," your specific instance might be "being alone on my first visit to a senior center in the neighborhood." By choosing a specific instance of a general type of situation, you make it more likely that you will become able to respond in a relaxed manner in specific situations that are problems for you.

COVERT REHEARSAL PRACTICE SCHEDULE

Date	Type of Situation	Specific Instance	Relaxation Response You Imagine	Positive Consequence of New Response

The third step in the covert rehearsal of relaxation responses is to DESCRIBE HOW YOU WANT TO REACT IN THE SITUA-TION. *This involves writing a brief discription of how you want to respond. You should include the word "relax" and any other things you might include to make a more comfortable, effective response.* For example, if you had described a specific instance such as "waiting for a bus," the reaction you describe might be "relax and read the newspaper." If your specific instance were "talk to my oldest son about his health," you might have as your reaction "Relax and ask him how he is currently feeling and what the doctor said at his last check-up." Specifying how you want to react prepares you to react comfortably in real life problem situations.

The fourth step in covertly practicing relaxation is to WRITE A POSITIVE CONSEQUENCE OF YOUR NEW REACTION. *This involves writing a very brief description of something positive which might happen as a result of your new reaction in the situation.* For example, if your new reaction is "to relax and talk to my friend," the positive consequence might be "she tells me something interesting." If your positive reaction is "relax and read a book," the positive consequence might be "I learned something that helps me in my life." By thinking of a positive consequence of your new reaction, you increase the liklihood that you will enjoy the new reaction you are imagining.

The fifth step in covert rehearsal for relaxed responses is to IMAGINE OR COVERTLY REHEARSE THE SEQUENCE YOU HAVE SPECIFIED. *To do this, imagine this sequence as vividly as you can: "specific instance—your reaction—the positive consequence."* Imagine the specific situation, and then imagine yourself relaxing and acting in just the way you want to. Try to see yourself doing this just as though you were there; don't just go through the motions—actually see yourself relaxing and reacting in the new way. As you imagine this sequence, you may want to practice very precisely what you do and how you do it and to experiment with what feels like the best way of doing it. Finally, imagine the positive consequence you specified. By covertly rehearsing this sequence, you make it much more likely that you will be comfortable and effective in the real life situation you are working on. This surprising effect of covert rehearsal has been shown in numerous studies in recent years.

The sixth step of the covert rehearsal of relaxation is to SPECIFY AND COVERTLY REHEARSE FURTHER RELAX-ATION SEQUENCES. *This involves repeating Steps 2 through 6 which we have just described.* For example, if the general type of situation you were working on was "talking to a new acquaintance" and you had just rehearsed a sequence involving talking to a friendly person your age, you would pick another instance of the same type of general situation. The second instance would be picked only after you had rehearsed the first sequence to your satisfaction. The second instance might be "unexpectedly running into a person I met the other day." You would then describe the way in which you wanted to react—for example, "relax and ask her how she has been"; and finally, you would devise a positive consequence of your new reaction such as "she smiles and tells me that she is glad to see me." Once you have specified this "instance—new reaction—positive consequence" sequence, you would proceed to covertly rehearse the sequence as described in Step No. 5. Once you are satisfied with your second sequence, go on to a third and fourth, etc. When you have rehearsed *all* of the specific instances of a type of situation you can think of, decide on a new type of situation and start to work on specific instances of that situation. By rehearsing many instances of one general type of situation, you build your capacity to behave comfortably and effectively in a wide variety of situations.

The seventh step in the covert practice of relaxed responses is to REPEAT STEPS ONE THROUGH SIX TWICE A DAY. *This means that you will do two covert practice sessions each day during your relaxation practice session.* This means that you may want to spend less time simply practicing relaxation in these sessions so that you will have time to do these exercises. By doing two sessions a day, you will slowly increase your ability to become relaxed and act effectively in a growing variety of situations.

In summary, the steps involved in covert practice of relaxed responses are as follows:

1. PICK A TYPE OF SITUATION YOU WANT TO WORK ON
2. CHOOSE A SPECIFIC INSTANCE OF THE TYPE OF SITUATION YOU WANT TO WORK ON
3. DESCRIBE HOW YOU WANT TO REACT IN THAT SITUATION
4. WRITE A POSITIVE CONSEQUENCE OF YOUR NEW REACTION
5. IMAGINE OR COVERTLY REHEARSE THE SEQUENCE YOU HAVE SPECIFIED
6. SPECIFY AND COVERTLY REHEARSE FURTHER RELAXATION SEQUENCES
7. REPEAT STEPS 1 THROUGH 6 TWICE A DAY

Relaxing in Actual Situations

After you have covertly rehearsed relaxation responses, you should begin to RELAX IN ACTUAL SITUATIONS. *This involves relaxing in real life situations that have typically made you uncomfortable.* By doing this, you will begin to be able to relax in situations that have been a problem to you.

During your first day of practicing relaxation in real life situations, you should RESPOND WITH RELAXATION AT LEAST TWICE. The two times that you relax in real life situations may be planned at the start of the day or can happen spontaneously as situations present themselves. However, you should plan *at least one relaxation response in advance of the situation.*

Whenever you practice relaxing in a real life situation, RECORD THE FACT THAT YOU RELAXED ON THE RECORDS YOU HAVE BEEN KEEPING. By recording relaxation you will be able to see the improvement you are making, and that will help us to make any modifications in this program that are needed.

In practicing in real life, you will undoubtedly find situations in which you are not as smooth or successful as you would like to be. When this happens, REHEARSE A BETTER RELAXATION RESPONSE IN YOUR NEXT COVERT REHEARSAL SESSION. Think about how you reacted in an actual situation. Was it satisfactory to you? If not, can you think of a better thing to say or a better way to react? If so, *try the modified relaxation response in your next imagination session and later in real life.*

Finally, INCREASE THE NUMBER OF TIMES YOU PRACTICE RELAXATION IN REAL LIFE BY ONE EACH DAY. *This means that on the third day you will be relaxing* at least four times, etc. If so, on the seventh day, you will be relaxing at least eight times.

In summary, the steps of actually relaxing in real life are as follows:

1. RELAX IN ACTUAL SITUATIONS
2. RESPOND WITH RELAXATION AT LEAST TWICE
3. RECORD THE FACT THAT YOU RELAXED ON THE RELAXATION LOG SHEETS YOU HAVE BEEN KEEPING
4. REHEARSE A BETTER RELAXATION RESPONSE IN YOUR NEXT COVERT REHEARSAL SESSION
5. INCREASE THE NUMBER OF TIMES YOU PRACTICE RELAXATION IN REAL LIFE BY ONE EACH DAY

APPENDIX 13

CREATING A PERSONAL PLAN
TO OVERCOME DEPRESSION

Up to this point in treatment you have learned two important skills to help you to overcome depression: monitoring mood and activities (both pleasant and unpleasant) and learning how to become more relaxed in real life situations. You may want to include a number of other skills in your personal plan for reducing and controlling depression.

Before going into these other skills, we would like to emphasize that the first step in developing your plan is to take stock of your problem areas and the skills you may need to deal with these problems. Once you have done this, you are ready to set up a program with your therapist's help. You will need to set priorities as to what problem(s) should be tackled first. Remember, it is wise to work on only one or two problems at a time; as you gain success with these, you can move on to others of lesser priority.

Let us return now to the areas you will need to look at.

1. Pleasant Activities

Many depressed persons, even at this point in treatment, are still doing fewer enjoyable things than they would like to do. They are often busy doing what they *have* to do, but have given up many things they *want* to do just for enjoyment. This probably still applies to you, and so you should continue tracking the frequency of pleasant and unpleasant events that occur and make an effort to increase positive experiences throughout the remainder of your therapy. While the *content* of the tracking sheets may change, the *idea* is still a good one to pursue.

2. Relaxation

Do you think of yourself as a tense, anxious person most of the time? (Try to answer in terms of whether you actually *feel relaxed* most of the time; this is different from simply having mastered techniques of *how* to relax.) Most persons still have room for improvement in this regard, and so we recommend that you continue daily practice of relaxation techniques, both in your imagination and in real life situations, for the remainder of treatment. This skill will come in handy as you zero in on other more personal issues, and should help you to progress faster.

3. Problems Being Direct and Assertive with People

Many depressed persons have difficulty behaving in an assertive way, particularly toward those friends or relatives with whom they have a close relationship. It may, for example, be relatively easy for you to return bad merchandise to a store, but a lot more difficult to express your feelings to those on whom you depend for various things. Being "assertive" covers a broad category of circumstances. It includes things like saying "no" when that is what you mean, speaking up when asked for your opinion, being able to disagree, and being able to express both positive and negative feelings to others without feeling guilty or embarrassed. If you lack these skills, you may want to focus on assertion training with your therapist.

4. Problems with Negative Thinking

Many depressed persons are troubled by frequent self-critical, pessimistic thoughts about themselves and their experiences. A number of professionals in the field of psychology think that these kinds of thoughts are directly responsible for depression. For example, do you expect that most situations will have a negative outcome, even when there is no really good reason to think this? Do you frequently regard yourself as a failure and worry about all the things you should have done? Do you often think about horrible things that may happen to you and then find that you can't turn off these thoughts?

Don't become too discouraged if you have said "yes" to several of the above questions. There are techniques available to help you modify these thinking patterns. Your therapist can help you learn a number of skills to control and change your habits of thinking. However, you will have to work hard at this, because these thoughts are usually so automatic and deeply ingrained that it takes considerable effort and time to change them.

5. Problems Communicating with Others

A very important factor to consider in your personal plan is how you come across to others. If you have difficulty in establishing pleasant relationships with others, then this may affect your ability to change environmental events or relationships that are contributing to your depression. It is a good idea to find out whether others find it pleasant or unpleasant to associate with you as well as what aspects of your personal style might be contributing to this. There are a number of unpleasant mannerisms that many depressed individuals develop, and these often can be instrumental in making communication with others occur less often and be more negative. For example, depressed persons often have slow, halting speech, are unresponsive in conversations, show little interest in others, avoid eye contact when talking, and so forth. They also are critical of themselves and others as reflected in complaining, brooding out loud, etc. Frequently they "let themselves go" in appearance, and scowls and frowns occur more often than smiles.

Taking time to evaluate with your therapist whether you have any of these mannerisms and then setting up plans to change them will be a sound step toward more pleasant interactions with others. It is difficult at times for us to see ourselves as others see us. It is even harder to change these verbal and/or non-verbal habits once identified. However, working systematically at this process of self-change will effect changes in the way others relate to you; this in turn will greatly help you to improve your self-image.

Self-Control Problems

Despite good intentions and a willingness to change, many depressed persons find it difficult to really get down to work on their problems. In the course of your therapy thus far, you have probably identified two or three areas you want to change in yourself. The question now is: do you have sufficient energy and commitment to do so? Often tiredness, lack of interest, and discouragement accompany depression, and it is easy to feel like quitting therapy or abandoning your plan for self-improvement when such feelings are present. Fortunately, they tend to come and go; this means you can learn to take advantage of the "good" days, begin to have some success, and then encourage yourself to keep on working even when you feel "lousy."

Self-instructional techniques—ways of silently talking to yourself (like being your own "coach") in tough situations can be very helpful in this regard. When used appropriately, self-talk helps to guide our behavior, gives us a sense of direction, and encourages us to keep on track. If you tend to start things and then drop them, or to disengage when you feel even a little depressed, you probably can benefit from a program designed to improve your self-control skills. It makes sense to focus on this area (if it is appropriate) *before* working on other problems, since both sustained effort and hard work are needed to make lasting changes in any of the other problem areas you have been thinking about.

Final Comment

Try to approach taking stock and creating a personal plan to overcome depression in a *constructive* way. Don't browbeat yourself for having more problems to work on, and don't try to work on all of them at once. It took time to get into the net of depression, and it will take time and effort to change your habits and get out of the rut. Try to keep a perspective on yourself as you tackle these more difficult skills for change. Measure your progress often, and give yourself a pat on the back for even small changes. In this way you will be building in skills to handle new problems that may arise later on when therapy is over.

APPENDIX 14

SKILL TRAINING SITUATION*

Please relate a concrete situation that is an example of the area of skill training on which you and your therapist will focus.

1. Definition of situation

    A. Event(s) relate to problem that is/are occurring, and are unpleasant and aversive: _____

    _____

    _____

    _____

    B. *When* does the situation occur?: _____

    _____

    _____

    C. *Where* does it occur? (describe) _____

    _____

    _____

    D. *With whom* does it happen? _____

    _____

    E. *How often* does it occur? _____

    _____

2. Describe responses in situation.

    A. What do I do? _____

    _____

    _____

    B. What do I say? _____

    _____

*Adapted from Lewinsohn & Grosscup, 1978.

C. What do I think? _____

_____

D. How do I feel? _____

_____

E. What do others do in the situation? _____

_____

3. Possible solutions:

A. What might I do differently? _____

_____

_____

B. What might I say differently? _____

_____

C. How might I think differently? _____

_____

4. What would the possible end result be if I tried these solutions?

_____

_____

_____

5. What skill(s) do I need to learn or work on to decrease the aversiveness or the occurrence of this problem, or to increase the enjoyability and occurrence of this situation?

_____

_____

_____

_____

_____

APPENDIX 15

DAILY PLAN SHEETS

Part 1. Usual Daily Activities

Routine Activities	"Have To" Activities	"Want To" Activities
1.	1.	1.
2.	2.	2.
3.	3.	3.
4.	4.	4.
5.	5.	5.
6.	6.	6.
7.	7.	7.
8.	8.	8.
9.	9.	9.
10.	10.	10.
11.	11.	11.
12.	12.	12.

DAILY PLAN SHEETS

Part 2. Daily Plan

	Monday	Tuesday	Wednesday	Thursday	Friday	Saturday	Sunday
7:00							
8:00							
9:00							
10:00							
11:00							
12:00							
1:00							
2:00							
3:00							
4:00							
5:00							
6:00							
7:00							
8:00							
9:00